GRILLED SEAFOOD COOKBOOK

Tasty and Easy to Follow Recipes to Grill Your Favourite Foods

(How to Prepare Easy and Flavorful Grilled Recipes)

Nadia Brunson

Published by Sharon Lohan

© **Nadia Brunson**

All Rights Reserved

Grilled Seafood Cookbook: Tasty and Easy to Follow Recipes to Grill Your Favourite Foods (How to Prepare Easy and Flavorful Grilled Recipes)

ISBN 978-1-990334-82-5

All rights reserved. No part of this guide may be reproduced in any form without permission in writing from the publisher except in the case of brief quotations embodied in critical articles or reviews.

Legal & Disclaimer

The information contained in this book is not designed to replace or take the place of any form of medicine or professional medical advice. The information in this book has been provided for educational and entertainment purposes only.

The information contained in this book has been compiled from sources deemed reliable, and it is accurate to the best of the Author's knowledge; however, the Author cannot guarantee its accuracy and validity and cannot be held liable for any errors or omissions. Changes are periodically made to this book. You must consult your doctor or get professional medical advice before using any of the suggested remedies, techniques, or information in this book.

Table of contents

Part 1 1
1. 25-Minute Grilled Pork Chops with Succotash 2
2. Amazing 'Pizza' Pork Chops Recipe 5
3. Andrew's Favorite Grilled Pork Chops Recipe 7
Apple Glazed Pork Recipe 9
Pricot Habanero Pork Chops 11
Asian Marinated Pork Chops 13
Bada Bing Pork Chops Recipe 15
Basil-Garlic Grilled Pork Chops 17
Beer Brined Pork Chops 18
Best Grilled Pork Chops 20
Best Pork Chop Marinade 21
Bone-In Pork Milanese with Soy-Honey Glaze 23
Bourbon Glazed Pork Chops 25
Brined Pork Chops with Soft Parmigiano Polenta 26
Butterflied Cuban Style Pork Chops 29
Cheesy Pork Chops with Spicy Apples 31
Cherry Chutney Grilled Chops 33
Chesapeake Bay Pork Chops 35
Chili-Rubbed Pork Chops 37
Chinese Pork Chops 39
Chipotle Orange Glazed Pork Chops 40
Cider Brined Grilled Stuffed Pork Chops 41
Citrus Grilled Pork Filet with Mint Fig Sauce 44
Citrus Marinated Cuban Pork Chops 46

Cold Smoked Maple-Balsamic Glazed Pork Chops 48
Country Mustard Rubbed Pork Chops 50
Delicious Tangy Pork Chops Recipe 51
Dijon Grilled Pork Chops Recipe 52
Double Thick Grilled Pork Chop with Ginger Plum Bbq Sauce 54
Early Autumn Smoked Pork Chops 57
Easy Grilled Pork Chops 59
Emeril's Shake 'Em Up Pork Chops 61
Fabienne's Grilled Center Cut Pork Chops Recipe 64
Filipino Grilled Pork Chops 66
Fontina and Prosciutto Stuffed Pork Chops with Grilled Polenta Squares and Roasted California Grapes 68
Glazed Grilled Pork Chops Recipe 71
Grilled 'Fusion' Pork Chops Recipe 73
Grilled Apple Brined Pork Chops 74
Grilled Asian Ginger Pork Chops 76
Grilled Berkshire Pork Chop with Merlot Sauce 77
Grilled Bone-In Pork Chops 79
Grilled Bone-in Pork Chops with Hawaiian Marinade 80
Grilled Brown Sugar Pork Chops 82
Grilled Corn Salad with Lime, Red Chili and Cotija 84
Grilled Giant Pork Chops with Sweet Peach Barbecue Sauce 85
Grilled Hoisin Pork Chop Noodle Bowl 88
Grilled Italian Pork Chops 91
Grilled Jamaican Jerked Pork Loin Chops 92
Grilled Korean-Style BBQ Glazed Pork Chops with Red Onions and Baby Bok Choy 94

Grilled Lemon Herb Pork Chops	96
Grilled Mongolian Pork Chops Recipe	97
Honey Mustard BBQ Pork Chops Recipe	100
Honey Mustard Dream Delight Pork Chops	102
Part 2	104
Classic/Boring Grilled Cheese	105
Tomato and Basil Grilled Cheese	106
Tomato and Bacon	107
Leftover Jalapeno	108
Grilled Cheese Fingers	109
The Creamy Red Goat	110
Spicy Mayo Thing	111
Sriracha Mayo Grilled Cheese	112
Pesto Tomato	113
Havarti and Seafood Salad	114
Garlic Bread and Cheese	115
Guacamole and Stuff	116
Movie Popcorn Grilled Cheese	117
Mushrooms and Swiss Cheese	118
Rabbi's Delight	119
Cajun Shrimp	120
Roasted Tomatoes	121
Blue Cheese Pony Express	122
Italian Gangster Sandwich	123
Gandalf Grilled Cheese	124
Mediterranean Grilled Cheese	125
Zeus's Favorite Sandwich	126

Jalapeno Popper 127

Roast Beast.. 128

On the Subject of Hamburger Buns...................................... 129

This Recipe is Gonna Blow Your Mind (Macaroni and Ground Beef)... 130

Hot Dogs and Maple Syrup.. 131

Leftover Pizza Grilled Cheese... 132

Green Olives and Mozzarella.. 133

Big City Waffle 134

Canadian Senator... 135

Fat Hawaiian 136

Somebody Left a Baguette at my Party and I Don't Know What to do with it... 137

Brie and Marmalade.. 138

Apples, Bacon, and Brie 139

Obese American Doughnut.. 140

Pulled Pork Grilled Cheese 141

You ever buy too much breakfast at McDonald's?.............. 142

Teriyaki Grilled Cheese 143

Green Herbs and White Cheese... 144

Chipotle Meat.. 145

On the Subject of Beavers 146

Vegan Grilled Cheese... 147

Blueberries and Maple Syrup... 148

Actually a Pulled Pork Sandwich... 149

You know you can swap out some of these ingredients, right? 150

German Drunkfest.. 151

Ghetto Lobster Roll	152
Anchovies and Mozzarella	153
Sides to Serve with Grilled Cheese	154
Instant Pot BBQ Pork	155
Kansas City Style Pork Ribs	158
No-Fuss Baked Baby Back Ribs	161
Oven Barbecue Pork Ribs Recipe	164
Prize Winning Baby Back Ribs Recipe	167
Recipe: Oven-Baked Barbecue Ribs	169
Rhubarb-Apricot Barbecued Chicken	171
Slow Cooker Barbecue Ribs	173
Southern Grilled Barbecued Ribs Recipe	175
Spicy and Sticky Baby Back Ribs	177
Stickiest ever BBQ ribs with chive dip recipe	179
Texas Pork Ribs Recipe	182
The Best BBQ Chicken Breasts	185
The Ultimate Barbecued Chicken	187
The Ultimate Barbecued Ribs	190

Part 1

1. 25-Minute Grilled Pork Chops with Succotash

Ingredients:

2 medium yellow tomatoes, cut into 1/2-inch thick wedges (about 1 pound)
kosher salt and freshly ground black pepper
1/2 cup sour cream
zest and juice of 1 lime
1/4 teaspoon cumin
1/4 cup extra-virgin olive oils, plus more for oiling the grill grates
4 bone-in pork chops, 1-inch thick (about 3 pounds)
4 ears yellow corn, shucked
1 large red onion, sliced into 1/2-inch rounds (about 8 ounces)
ounce one 15- can black-eyed peas, drained and rinsed
1/2 cup roughly-chopped fresh parsley

Directions:

Make a grill or large grill pan for medium-high heat.

Put the tomatoes right into a sizable mixing bowl. Sprinkle with salt and pepper and let sit at room temperature when you prepare all those other

Ingredients. Put the sour cream, lime zest and juice, cumin and a pinch of salt and pepper in a little bowl and whisk to combine. Reserve.

Lightly oil the grill grates. Brush the pork around with 2 tablespoons of the oil and sprinkle liberally with salt and pepper. Arrange the pork using one side of the grill (leave room for grilling the vegetables) and cook until lightly charred on both sides and an instant-read thermometer inserted into the deepest part of a chop registers 140 degrees F, about 5 minutes per side. Remove from the grill and let rest for 5 minutes before serving.

Meanwhile, brush the corn and onion liberally with all of those other 2 tablespoons oil, sprinkle with salt and pepper and arrange them on the grill. Cook the corn until lightly charred, 6 to 8 8 minutes, rotating the ears so that they cook evenly. Cook the onion until charred and tender, 6 to 8 8 minutes, flipping as needed. Transfer the vegetables to a cutting board and cool for 2-3 3 minutes. When cool enough to deal with, slice the corn from the cobs and quarter the onion rounds. Add the corn, onion, black-eyed peas and half of the parsley to the same large bowl with the tomatoes. Gently toss to combine. Season to taste with salt and pepper.

Divide the succotash among 4 large dinner plates and top with a dollop of the reserved sour cream mixture. Place 1 pork chop on each plate next to the succotash.

Garnish the succotash with the reserved parsley and serve immediately.

2. Amazing 'Pizza' Pork Chops Recipe

Ingredients:

5 eaches boneless pork chops
1 pinch salt and ground black pepper to taste
5 slices tomato (1/2-inch thick)
1/4 cup chopped fresh basil
1 tablespoon chopped fresh oregano
2 cloves garlic , minced
2 tablespoons olive oil
5 slices mozzarella cheese

Directions:

Step one 1 Preheat a patio grill for medium heat.

Step two 2 Season the pork chops with salt and black pepper and arrange in underneath of a disposable aluminum pan; top each with a tomato slice. Divide the basil, oregano, and garlic between your pork chops; drizzle with the essential olive oil. Cover the pan with aluminum foil.

Step three 3 Cook on the preheated grill before pork is no more pink in the guts, about 25 minutes. An instant-read thermometer inserted in to the center should read 145 degrees F (63 degrees C). Take away the pan from the grill; top each pork chop with a slice of mozzarella cheese, replace the aluminum foil over the pan, and wait before cheese melts, three to five five minutes, before serving.

3. Andrew's Favorite Grilled Pork Chops Recipe

Ingredients:

1 cup orange juice
1/3 cup reduced-sodium soy sauce
1/4 cup olive oil
2 teaspoons minced fresh rosemary
2 eaches green onions, sliced
4 eaches thick-cut boneless center cut pork chops

Directions:

The first step Blend the orange juice, soy sauce, olive oil, rosemary, and green onions in a huge plastic freezer bag; place the chops into the bag, squeeze away the air, and seal the handbag. Refrigerate to marinate 8 hours or overnight.

Step two The next day, preheat a garden barbeque grill for medium temperature, and lightly essential oil the grate.

Step three Remove the grinds from the salatsoße, and discard the used marinade. Move excess marinade from the chops, and grill until pig is browned, no longer pink inside, and shows good grill marks, about 15 minutes per side. An instant-read meat thermometer put into the thicker part of a chop should read at least 145 degrees F (63 degrees C)

Apple Glazed Pork Recipe

Ingredients:

4 eaches granny smith apples , cored and chopped
1 (8-ounce) can crushed pineapple , with juice
1/2 cup apple cider vinegar
1/4 cup brown sugar
1/4 cup dijon mustard
1/4 cup water
2 tablespoons honey
4 cloves garlic , crushed
2 teaspoons cayenne pepper
1 teaspoon onion powder
6 raw chop with refuse, 113 g; (blank) 4 ounces boneless pork chops

Directions:

The first step Place apples, pineapple and juice, vinegar, glucose, mustard, water, honies, garlic, cayenne, and onion powder in a sizable saucepan. Provide to a over-heat high heat, after that reduce heat to medium-low, cover, and simmer until the apples are sensitive, about 15 a few minutes. Allow the mix to cool to room temperature, after that puree in a blender until soft. Place the chicken chops to a resealable plastic bag, and pour the apple puree overtop. Marinate in the refrigerator overnight.

Stage 2 Preheat an outdoor grill for moderate heat, and gently oil grate. Remove pork chops from marinade, and wring off excess. Eliminate remaining marinade.

Stage 3 Cook upon preheated grill till the chops shall no longer end up being pink in the centre, about five minutes per aspect according to the width.

Pricot Habanero Pork Chops

Ingredients:

4 bone-in center-cut pork chops
kosher salt and freshly ground black pepper
1 cup apricot preserves
2 tablespoons soy sauce
1 tablespoon grated ginger
2 cloves garlic , grated on a rasp grater
1 orange , zested and juiced
1/2 to 1 habanero pepper, seeded and diced
vegetable oil , for the grill grates
1 tablespoon chopped fresh mint
1 green apple , peeled, cored and finely diced
1 red bell pepper, finely diced
1 scallion, thinly sliced on the bias
1 lime, zested and juiced

Directions:

For the pork chops: Season the pork chops with salt and pepper; reserve while making the glaze.

Add the apricot preserves, soy sauce, ginger, garlic, orange zest and juice and habanero to a tiny pot and bring to a simmer. Simmer before sauce is reduced and thickened, 10 to a quarter-hour; let cool. Divide the glaze between 2 bowls, reserving 1 bowl for basting and one for serving with the cooked chops.

Preheat a grill to medium-high heat. Coat the grates with a good amount of vegetable oil to greatly help create a nonstick surface.

Utilizing a brush, coat the chops with the first round of glaze. Place them on the grill glazed-side down and grill without moving before glaze commences to caramelize, about five minutes. Brush the tops with glaze, flip the chops, brush the other side with an increase of glaze and continue cooking before chops are caramelized, charred and sticky and the inner temperature registers 135 degrees F, another 7 to ten minutes. Discard the basting glaze. Allow chops rest for 5 to ten minutes, coating them once with the reserved serving glaze while resting.

For the relish: Combine the mint, apple, bell pepper, scallion and lime zest and juice in a bowl and toss to coat.

Top the pork chops with some green apple relish and serve with the rest of the serving glaze and relish.

Asian Marinated Pork Chops

Ingredients:

1 cup soy sauce
1/2 cup brown sugar
2 cloves garlic , crushed
1 tablespoon ground ginger
1 tablespoon ground cumin
1 tablespoon roasted red chili paste
6 (1-inch thick) pork chops

Directions:

Step one 1 Place the soy sauce, brown sugar, garlic, ginger, cumin, and chili paste in a big, heavy plastic zipper bag. Smush the bag several times with your fingers to combine all of the Ingredients. thoroughly and dissolve the brown sugar; place the pork chops in to the marinade, and seal the bag. Allow to marinate for 30 to 45 minutes.

Step two 2 Preheat a patio grill for medium heat, and lightly oil the grate.

Step 3 3 Take away the pork chops from the marinade, and discard the marinade. Get rid of excess marinade, and grill the pork chops until browned, the meat is no more pink inside, and the chops show good grill marks,

5 to 7 minutes per side. An instant-read meat thermometer inserted in to the thickest part of a chop should read at least 145 degrees F (63 degrees C).

Bada Bing Pork Chops Recipe

Ingredients:

1 cup salad dressing Italian-style salad dressing
1/2 cup Worcestershire sauce Worcestershire sauce
1/2 cup applesauce applesauce
1/4 cup hot pepper sauce hot pepper sauce
1 lime lime juiced
6 pork chops eaches bone-in pork chops

Directions:

Step one 1 Mix together the Italian dressing, Worcestershire sauce, applesauce, hot pepper sauce, and lime juice in a bowl. Pour the marinade over the pork chops, and refrigerate in marinade for 6 hours or overnight.

Step two 2 Preheat a patio grill for medium heat, and lightly oil the grate.

Step 3 3 Take away the chops from the marinade, and pour marinade right into a saucepan. Bring the marinade to a boil over medium heat, and invite to boil for approximately 1 minute. Place the pork chops onto the preheated grill, and grill until well browned no longer pink in the centre, about 6 minutes per side, basting the chops occasionally with the marinade. An instant-read thermometer inserted in to the center should read 145 degrees F (63 degrees C). Permit the marinade baste to cook completely onto the chops.

Basil-Garlic Grilled Pork Chops

Ingredients:

    4 (8 ounce) pork chops
    1 lime, juiced
    4 cloves garlic , minced
    1/4 cup chopped fresh basil
    1 pinch salt and black pepper to taste

Directions:

Step one 1 Toss the pork chops with the lime juice in a bowl until evenly covered. Toss with garlic and basil. Season the chops to taste with salt and pepper. Reserve to marinate for thirty minutes.

Step two 2 Preheat a patio grill for medium heat, and lightly oil the grate.

Step three 3 Cook the pork chops on the preheated grill until no more pink in the guts, 5 to ten minutes per side. An instant-read thermometer inserted in to the center should read 145 degrees F (63 degrees C).

Beer Brined Pork Chops

Ingredients:

1 can beer (12 ounce) beer
1 tablespoon red wine vinegar red wine vinegar
3 tablespoons corn syrup dark corn syrup
2 tablespoons mustard prepared mustard
4 cloves garlic large garlic minced
1 teaspoon sage dried sage
1 tablespoon salt salt
1 tablespoon black pepper ground black pepper
1 slice onion small onion cut into thick
8 pork chops eaches (1-inch thick) center-cut pork chops

Directions:

Step one 1 Whisk the beer, wine vinegar, corn syrup, mustard, garlic, sage, salt, and black pepper together in a bowl; pour right into a resealable plastic bag. Add the onion and pork chops, coat with the marinade, squeeze out excess air, and seal the bag. Marinate in the refrigerator for 12 hours.

Step two 2 Preheat a patio grill for medium heat, and lightly oil the grate.

Step 3 3 Take away the pork chops and onions from the marinade and reserve on a platter. Drain the marinade through a fine-mesh strainer, discarding the strained liquid. Spread the garlic mixture caught in the strainer over the pork chops. Wrap the onions in aluminum foil.

Step 4 Cook the packet of onions and the pork chops on the preheated grill before pork is no more pink in the guts, about 7 minutes per side. An instant-read thermometer inserted in to the center should read 145 degrees F (63 degrees C).

Best Grilled Pork Chops

Ingredients:

1/2 cup water
1/3 cup light soy sauce
1/4 cup vegetable oil
3 tablespoons lemon pepper seasoning
2 teaspoons minced garlic
6 eaches boneless pork loin chops, trimmed of fat

Directions:

Step one 1 Mix water, soy sauce, vegetable oil, lemon pepper seasoning, and minced garlic in a deep bowl; add pork chops and marinate in refrigerator at least 2 hours.

Step two 2 Preheat a patio grill for medium-high heat and lightly oil the grate.

Step three 3 Remove pork chops from the marinade and get rid of excess. Discard the rest of the marinade.

Step 4 Cook the pork chops on the preheated grill until no more pink in the guts, 5 to 6 minutes per side. An instant-read thermometer inserted in to the center should read 145 degrees F (63 degrees C).

Best Pork Chop Marinade

Ingredients:

2 large (blank)s large pork chops
1/4 cup extra-virgin olive oil
3 tablespoons dark brown sugar
2 tablespoons lemon juice
2 tablespoons spicy brown mustard
4 cloves garlic , chopped
2 teaspoons dried thyme
1 teaspoon onion powder
1 teaspoon worcestershire sauce
1 teaspoon white wine vinegar
1 teaspoon mesquite-flavored seasoning
1/2 teaspoon dried parsley flakes
1/2 teaspoon kosher salt
1/2 teaspoon freshly ground black pepper

Directions:

Step one 1 Cut each pork chop in one side through the center horizontally to within 1/2 inch of the other side. Open both sides and spread them out as an open book.

Step two 2 Whisk essential olive oil, brown sugar, lemon juice, mustard, garlic, thyme, onion powder, Worcestershire sauce, vinegar, mesquite seasoning, parsley, salt, and pepper together in a bowl and pour into a sizable resealable plastic bag. Add pork chops, coat with the marinade, squeeze out excess air, and seal the bag. Marinate in the refrigerator, six to eight 8 hours.

Bone-In Pork Milanese with Soy-Honey Glaze

Ingredients:

2 tablespoons canola oil
1 large shallot, thinly sliced
pinch red pepper flakes
1 tablespoon rice wine vinegar
1/2 cup honey
1/2 cup soy sauce
salt and freshly ground black pepper
4 bone-in center cut pork chops , pounded thin between 2 pieces of plastic wrap
canola oil
salt and freshly ground black pepper
soy-honey glaze
chopped green onions , for garnish

Directions:

For the glaze:

Heat the oil in a tiny saucepan over medium heat. Add the shallot and cook until soft. Stir in debt pepper flakes and cook for 30 seconds.

Deglaze the pan with rice wine vinegar, and stir in the honey and soy and cook until just heated through.

Remove from heat and season with pepper, to taste. Transfer to a bowl and let cool to room temperature.

For the pork chop:

Heat the grill to high. Brush the chops with oil on both sides and season with salt and pepper. Grill until golden brown on both sides, and just cooked through, brushing with a number of the glaze, about three minutes per side. Remove to a platter, brush with an increase of of the glaze and garnish with green onions.

Bourbon Glazed Pork Chops

Ingredients:

2 tablespoons dijon mustard
1 teaspoon packed dark brown sugar
1 tablespoon bourbon
pound two 1- center-cut bone-in pork chops , 1 1/2-inches thick
1 clove garlic , minced
the lady's house seasoning , as needed, recipe follows
1 cup salt
1/4 cup black pepper
1/4 cup garlic powder

Directions:

Make a medium-hot grill.

In a bowl, mix together the mustard, brown sugar, and bourbon. Rub the pork chops with the garlic and house seasoning, then brush with half the glaze.

Place the chops on the grill. Grill before chops are slightly charred and cooked, about 20 minutes. Brush with the rest of the glaze before serving.

Mix the Ingredients together and store within an airtight container for 6 months.

Brined Pork Chops with Soft Parmigiano Polenta

Ingredients:

1/2 cup salt , or to taste
1/3 cup sugar
2 tablespoons fennel seed
2 tablespoons coriander seed
1 teaspoon crushed red pepper flakes
3 bay leaves
1 onion , diced
2 carrots, peeled and diced
2 ribs celery , diced
4 cloves garlic smashed
1 1/2 quarts cold water
4 bone- in pork rib chops
1 tablespoon wild fennel pollen*
soft parmigiano polenta, recipe follows
1 1/2 cups milk
1 1/2 cups water
1 bay leaf
salt
1 cup long cooking polenta
1/2 cup grated parmigiano
1/4 cup mascarpone cheesesoft parmigiano polenta:

Directions:

For the brine: To help make the brine: In a huge container, add all the Ingredients: and stir to mix. Submerse the pork chops in the brine and refrigerate for 3 days. After 3 days take away the chops from the brine, discarding the brine. Preheat a grill or grill pan. Roll the fat edge of every pork chop with the fennel pollen. Place porks chop gently on the preheated grill or grill pan. After three to four 4 minutes rotate the chops 90 degrees to create lovely grill marks. Grill the chops for another three to four 4 minutes and start and repeat the procedure. If the chops seem to be to be burning move the chops to a cooler section of the grill to permit for longer cooking time without burning. Stand the chops up therefore the fat edge is in touch with the grill to crisp up the fat edge, this may also make the fennel pollen very aromatic. Take away the chops from the grill and let rest in a warm place before serving. The doneness of the meat ought to be about medium to medium well and incredibly juicy. Serve with polenta.

In a medium size saucepan, bring the milk, water and bay leaf to a boil. Season generously with salt, almost to the idea of over seasoning. How can you know that you is there? TASTE IT! When it has already reached a boil, slowly whisk in the polenta in small sprinkles. Once all the polenta has been incorporated, reduce heat to medium and immediately switch to stirring with a wooden spoon. Cook the polenta for 30 to 40 minutes, adding water if the polenta becomes too thick to loosen it up.

When the polenta is thoroughly cooked, it will look creamy rather than feel gritty on your own tongue. Take it off from heat and stir in the Parmigiano and mascarpone. Serve it immediately, or place a sheet of plastic wrap directly on the top of polenta to avoid a skin from forming at the top.

To reheat: Put in a little water to the polenta and heat over low to medium heat stirring constantly to avoid burning.

Butterflied Cuban Style Pork Chops

Ingredients:

3/4 cup fresh orange juice
1/2 cup fresh lime juice
1/3 cup coarsely chopped fresh oregano leaves
6 cloves garlic , coarsely chopped
1 teaspoon ground cumin
1/4 cup canola oil
4 (8-ounce) pork chops , butterflied and thinly pounded
salt and freshly ground black pepper
8 (1/4-inch) thick slices swiss cheese
8 (1/4-inch) thick slices boiled ham
2 sour dill pickles , thinly sliced (need about 16 slices)
2 tablespoons chopped cilantro leaves
1/4 cup olive oil

Directions:

Heat the grill to high. Whisk together 1/2 cup orange juice, 1/4 cup lime juice, 3 tablespoons oregano, the garlic, cumin, and canola oil in a huge baking dish. Add the pork and turn to coat. Cover and let marinate for at least quarter-hour or more to 2 hours in the refrigerator.

Take away the pork from the marinade and pat dry. Place the chops on a set surface, cut-side up and season with salt and pepper. Place 1 slice of cheese, 2 slices of ham, a few slices of pickle and another slice of cheese on 1 half of the chop. Fold over brush the very best with oil and season with salt and pepper. Repeat with remaining Ingredients. Place the chops on the grill, oil side down and grill until golden brown, three to four 4 minutes. Flip the chops over and continue grilling before bottom is golden brown and the cheese has melted, 2-3 3 minutes longer.

Whisk the rest of the orange and lime juices, oregano, and the cilantro with the essential olive oil and salt and pepper, to taste. Spoon over the chops and serve.

Cheesy Pork Chops with Spicy Apples

Ingredients:

1 tablespoon butter
1 onion , sliced
1 pinch red pepper flakes
1 apple , cored and sliced
2 teaspoons white sugar
2 tablespoons balsamic vinegar
4 pork chops
salt and pepper to taste
4 slices extra sharp Cheddar cheese

Directions:

Make a grill for high temperature.

As the grill heats, melt the butter in a skillet over medium heat. Add the onion, and cook until soft. Season with red pepper flakes then add the sliced apple. Stir in the sugar and balsamic vinegar, and simmer for five minutes, or until apples are soft and golden.

Season the pork chops with salt and pepper. Grill for three to five five minutes per side, according to thickness. Spoon the onions and apples along with the chops, and top with a slice of Cheddar cheese. Cover the grill, and cook for approximately three minutes until cheese is melted and bubbling.

Cherry Chutney Grilled Chops

Ingredients:

2 cups cider vinegar
2 teaspoons salt
1 teaspoon garlic powder
1 teaspoon dried basil
1/2 teaspoon crushed red pepper flakes
8 eaches bone-in pork chops
1 (12-ounce) package frozen black cherries, thawed
1 cup water
1/2 cup white sugar
2 tablespoons chopped fresh mint

Directions:

Step one 1 Whisk together the vinegar, salt, garlic powder, basil, and red pepper flakes in a sizable glass or ceramic bowl. Add the pork chops and toss to coat. Cover the bowl with plastic wrap; marinate in the refrigerator 6 hours to overnight.

Step two 2 Preheat a patio grill for medium-high heat; lightly oil the grate.

Step 3 3 As the grill heats, incorporate the cherries, water, and sugar in a saucepan over medium-low heat.

Cook, stirring occasionally, before sugar dissolves completely, 5 to ten minutes.

Step 4 4 Take away the pork chops from the marinade and get rid of excess moisture. Discard the rest of the marinade.

Step 5 Cook the pork chops on the preheated grill until no more pink in the guts, 8 to ten minutes per side. An instant-read thermometer inserted in to the center should read 160 degrees F (70 degrees C).

Step 6 Drizzle the chutney over the pork chops; garnish with the mint.

Chesapeake Bay Pork Chops

Ingredients:

1/2 cup vegetable oil
1/2 cup apple cider vinegar
1 tablespoon seafood seasoning
2 cloves minced garlic
1 tablespoon chopped fresh basil
1 lime, juiced
1 teaspoon cracked black pepper to taste
8 eaches boneless pork chops, 1/2 inch thick

Directions:

Step one 1 Whisk together the vegetable oil, apple cider vinegar, seafood seasoning, minced garlic, basil, lime juice, and black pepper in a bowl, and pour right into a resealable plastic bag. Add the pork chops, coat with the marinade, squeeze out excess air, and seal the bag. Marinate in the refrigerator for four to six 6 hours, flipping periodically.

Step two 2 Preheat a patio grill for medium-high heat, and lightly oil the grate. Take away the pork chops from the bags. Discard excess marinade.

Step three 3 Grill before pork is no more pink in the guts, 5 to 7 minutes per side. An instant-read thermometer inserted in to the center should read 145 degrees F (63 degrees C).

Chili-Rubbed Pork Chops

Ingredients:

2 large onions
1/3 cup new mexico chili powder
kosher salt
1/2 teaspoon dried oregano
1/2 teaspoon ground cumin
1/4 teaspoon ground cloves
2 cloves garlic , smashed
8 thin-cut boneless pork chops (about 2 pounds total), trimmed
vegetable oil , for brushing
spanish rice, for serving (optional)

Directions:

Roughly chop 1/2 onion and place in a blender with the chili powder, 1 1/2 teaspoons salt, the oregano, cumin, cloves and garlic. Puree, adding about 1/3 cup water to create a thick paste.

Cut the remaining 1 1/2 onions into thin rings and place in a bowl with the chili puree and pork; toss to coat.

Lightly brush a huge cast-iron skillet or grill pan with vegetable oil and place over high temperature until almost smoking. Place 4 pork chops in the skillet and surround with half of the onions. Cook before pork starts to blacken externally and is cooked through, about 4 minutes per side. Repeat with the rest of the pork chops and onions. Serve with rice, if desired.

Chinese Pork Chops

Ingredients:

1/2 cup soy sauce
1/4 cup brown sugar
2 tablespoons lemon juice
1 tablespoon vegetable oil
1/2 teaspoon ground ginger
teaspoon ? garlic powder
6 raw chop with refuse, 151 g; (blank) 5.3 ounces boneless pork chops

Directions:

Step one 1 In a bowl, mix the soy sauce, brown sugar, lemon juice, vegetable oil, ginger, and garlic powder. Reserve a few of the mixture in another bowl for marinating during cooking. Pierce the pork chops on both sides with a fork, place in a huge resealable plastic bag, and cover with the rest of the marinade mixture. Refrigerate six to eight 8 hours.

Step two 2 Preheat the grill for high temperature.

Step three 3 Lightly oil the grill grate. Discard marinade, and grill pork chops six to eight 8 minutes per side, or even to desired doneness, marinating often with the reserved part of the marinade.

Chipotle Orange Glazed Pork Chops

Ingredients:

2 tablespoons maple syrup
2 tablespoons orange juice concentrate
1 teaspoon finely chopped seeded chipotle with
1/2 teaspoon adobo
4 (3/4-inch thick) center cut pork loin chops (about 8 ounces each)
1/2 teaspoon salt

Directions:

In a tiny bowl incorporate the maple syrup, orange juice concentrate and chipotle.

Preheat grill pan. Sprinkle both sides of the chops with salt. Brush 1 side of chops generously with glaze. Put on grill pan glaze side down. Brush other side with glaze. Cook three to four 4 minutes per side over medium-high heat.

Cider Brined Grilled Stuffed Pork Chops

Ingredients:

3 bone-in, or boneless pork chops, about 2 pounds total
4 cups apple cider
2 cups oatmeal stout or other dark beer
1/2 cup kosher salt
1/2 cup raw sugar
1 tablespoon chipotle chili powder
2 cups apple cider
1 1/2 apples (pink lady, honey crisps, or cameo) cored and sliced 1/4-inch thick, grilled, about 1 minute each side, and diced
1 tablespoon mesquite honey
1 teaspoon chipotle chili powder
1 teaspoon ground cinnamon
red chili caramelized pecans, recipe follows
1/2 pound white cane sugar
1/4 cup water
1 pound whole pecans
1 tablespoon vanilla extract
1 teaspoon red chili powder

Directions:

For the brine:

Combine all Ingredients in a sizable container with a good fitting lid.

Take the pork chops and insert a fillet knife in to the side of every pork chop. Create a 2-inch slice along the medial side moving your knife along the within of the chop creating a pocket. Take care not to pierce the outer sides of the chop. Place the pork chops in the brine for from one hour or up to a day in the refrigerator.

For the reduction:

Add the cider to a medium saucepan over medium heat. Cook the cider, skimming off any scum that involves the top, until is becomes syrupy and is reduced to about 1/4 cup.

For the stuffing:

Combine all of the Ingredients in a sizable bowl.

Preheat grill to high.

Take away the pork chops from the brine, rinse and pat dry with paper towels. Stuff the cavity with the apples and grill for approximately ten minutes on each side. Remove from grill to a serving platter and let rest for approximately ten minutes. Brush with the cider reduction, sprinkle with the chopped caramelized pecans and revel in!

In a heavy-bottomed pot, cook the sugar and water before temperature reaches 275 degrees F on a candy thermometer. Add the pecans and stir to coat with the sugar. After the sugar commences to caramelize add the vanilla extract and stir gently but constantly until fully caramelized. Pour onto a silpat lined baking sheet to let cool, then sprinkle with the red chili powder.

Citrus Grilled Pork Filet with Mint Fig Sauce

Ingredients:

1 cup orange juice
2 tablespoons olive oil
3 cloves garlic , minced
6 (6 ounce) boneless pork loin chops
6 slices applewood smoked bacon
6 eaches fresh figs
1 cup fresh mint leaves
1 tablespoon balsamic vinegar
3 tablespoons olive oil
1 tablespoon honey
½ cup orange juice
1 pinch sea salt and pepper to taste

Directions:

The first step 1 Whisk together 1 cup orange juice, 2 tablespoons coconut oil, and the minced garlic in a bowl; pour in to a resealable plastic bag. Add the pork chops, coat with the marinade, squeeze out excess air, and seal the bag. Marinate in the refrigerator for at least 8 hours.

Second step 2 Place the figs and mint leaves in to a blender, and blend until pureed. Add the balsamic vinegar, 3 tablespoons coconut oil, honey, and 1/2 cup orange juice to the blender, and puree until smooth and thick. Season to taste with sea salt and pepper, then reserve.

Third step 3 Preheat an outdoor patio grill for medium-high heat, and lightly oil the grate. Get rid of the pork from the marinade. Discard all of those other marinade. Wrap each pork chop with a slice of bacon, securing with toothpicks as necessary; season with salt and pepper.

Step 4 Grill the pork chops before pork is forget about pink in the guts, about 5 minutes per side. An instant-read thermometer inserted into the center should read 145 degrees F (63 degrees C). Pour the mint-fig sauce over the pork chops to serve.

Citrus Marinated Cuban Pork Chops

Ingredients:

2 fruit, (2-5/8" dia, sphere)s naval oranges , zested and juiced
2 fruit (2" dia)s limes, zested and juiced
5 cloves garlic
1/2 cup loosely packed cilantro leaves
1/2 cup extra-virgin olive oil
1 pinch kosher salt and pepper to taste
2 (1 1/2 inches thick) boneless pork chops
1 cup shredded swiss cheese
2 (3 ounce) ham steaks (1/4 inch thick)
2 eaches dill pickle slices

Directions:

The first step 1 Place the orange juice, orange zest, lime juice, lime zest, garlic, cilantro, and coconut oil straight into a blender. Season to taste with kosher salt and pepper, then puree until smooth. Pour half of the vinaigrette in to a resealable plastic bag. Refrigerate all of those other for use later as a sauce.

Second step 2 Cut each pork chop in a single side through the guts horizontally to within one-half inch of the other side. Open both sides and spread them out as an open book. Pound with a meat mallet to 1/4 inch thick, then place the pork chops into the bag with the marinade. Squeeze out any excess air, and refrigerate 4-6 6 hours.

Third step 3 Preheat an outdoor patio grill for medium-high heat, and lightly oil the grate. Get rid of the pork chops from the marinade, and remove excess. Discard all of those other marinade.

Step 4 Open the pork chops on your own work surface. Sprinkle 1/4 cup of the Swiss cheese on underneath half of each pork chop. Cover the cheese with the ham steaks, then fan the sliced pickles together with the ham steaks. Sprinkle all of those other Swiss cheese over the pickles. Fold the most known half of the pork chop over the filling, and secure with several toothpicks.

Step 5 Cook on the preheated grill before pork is forget about pink in the guts and the filling is hot, about 5 minutes per side. An instant-read thermometer inserted into the center of the filling should read 145 degrees F (63 degrees C). Serve with the reserved citrus vinaigrette drizzled overtop.

Cold Smoked Maple-Balsamic Glazed Pork Chops

Ingredients:

1 1/2 cups wood chips (hickory or applewood or mesquite), soaked in cold water for at least 30 minutes
4 (1-inch) bone-in center cut pork chops
1 cup balsamic vinegar
1/4 cup maple syrup
pinch allspice
salt and freshly ground black pepper
canola oil

Directions:

Preheat the oven to 400 degrees F. Take away the wood chips from the water and spread evenly in underneath of a roasting pan. Cover the most notable tightly with aluminum foil. Devote the oven before chips get hot and get started to smoke, about a quarter-hour.

Take away the pan from the oven and take away the foil from the pan. Put a baking rack inside pan and arrange the chops along with the rack, leaving a few inches of space between each one. Quickly cover with the foil again and let take a seat on your kitchen counter for 10 to a quarter-hour.

As the pork chops are smoking, put the vinegar in a tiny pan over high temperature and cook until reduced to 1/4 cup, about five minutes. Remove from heat and whisk in the maple syrup, allspice, and salt and pepper, to taste. Let cool slightly.

Heat a grill pan over medium-high heat. Brush the ridges with a number of the canola oil. Brush the chops on both sides with a number of the glaze and season with salt and pepper. Grill on both sides, brushing with an increase of of the glaze, until golden brown and slightly charred and cooked to medium doneness, about 7 minutes per side. Remove from the grill, loosely tent and let rest for five minutes. Transfer to a serving platter and serve.

Country Mustard Rubbed Pork Chops

Ingredients:

1/2 cup country dijon mustard
2 teaspoons herb garden seasoning
1 teaspoon crushed garlic
1 teaspoon honey
2 tablespoons freshly chopped parsley leaves
1 1/2 pounds thick-cut boneless pork loin chops

Directions:

In a tiny bowl, incorporate the mustard, plants seasoning, garlic, honey and chopped parsley. Reserve 1/4 cup of the rub for serving.

Transfer mustard mixture to a resealable plastic bag. Add the pork chops and thoroughly coat with the mustard mixture. Allow pork chops sit for at least five minutes or so long as overnight, in the refrigerator, before grilling.

Heat a grill pan over medium heat. Grill the chops for 6 to 7 minutes per side.

Transfer to a serving platter and serve sprinkled with the reserved rub.

Delicious Tangy Pork Chops Recipe

Ingredients:

4 eaches boneless pork chops
1/2 cup lemon juice
1/2 cup worcestershire sauce
1/2 cup vegetable oil
1 tablespoon minced garlic

Directions:

Step one 1 Combine the pork chops, lemon juice, Worcestershire sauce, vegetable oil, and garlic in a huge resealable plastic bag. Squeeze as much excess air from bag as possible. Marinate in refrigerator 4 to a day.

Step two 2 Preheat a patio grill for medium-high heat, and lightly oil the grate.

Step 3 3 Take away the pork chops from the marinade right to the grill. Discard the marinade.

Step 4 Cook before pork is no more pink in the guts, about five minutes per side. An instant-read thermometer inserted in to the center should read 145 degrees F (63 degrees C).

Dijon Grilled Pork Chops Recipe

Ingredients:

   6 tablespoons dijon mustard
   6 tablespoons brown sugar
   3 tablespoons unsweetened apple juice
   3 tablespoons worcestershire sauce
   4 (8 ounce) bone-in pork loin chops

Directions:

Step one 1 Mix mustard, brown sugar, apple juice, and Worcestershire sauce together in a bowl until marinade is smooth. Pour 2/3 the marinade into a sizable resealable plastic bag. Add pork chops, coat with marinade, squeeze out excess air, and seal the bag. Marinate in the refrigerator for 8 hours to overnight. Cover bowl with remaining marinade with plastic wrap and refrigerate.

Step two 2 Remove pork chops from marinade and discard bag and marinade.

Step three 3 Preheat grill for medium heat and lightly oil the grate.

Step 4 Cook the pork chops on the preheated grill, basting with reserved marinade, until no more pink in the guts, 4 to five minutes per side. An instant-read thermometer inserted in to the center should read 145 degrees F (63 degrees C). Let pork chops are a symbol of five minutes before serving.

Double Thick Grilled Pork Chop with Ginger Plum Bbq Sauce

Ingredients:

6 plums , peeled and quartered
2 ounces ginger
1 small clove of garlic , crushed and chopped
6 ounces hosin sauce , plus some for garnish
8 ounces lite brown sugar
8 ounces water
2 ounces soy sauce
1 ground piece star anise
2 ounces cider vinegar
2 scallions
pork loin
salt
1 tablespoon rice wine vinegar
½ teaspoon sesame oil
½ teaspoon chili flakes
3 ounces bean sprouts
½ pound carrots, julienned
½ pound cucumber , julienned
2 to 3 scallions
1 teaspoon salt
½ teaspoon sugar
1hinese pancakes

Directions:

Preperation of Ginger Plum BBQ Sauce: Simmer plums, ginger, 1 clove garlic, hoisin sauce, brown sugar, 2 tablespoons water, soy sauce, and star anise, 20 minutes or until plums are loose. Add vinegar and simmer, uncovered, stirring constantly until sauce thickens, about ten minutes. Discard star anise, strain and stir in scallions.

Preparation of Meat: Trim loin into double thick chops, marinate in BBQ sauce overnight, and grill to desired temperature.

Preparation of Mushu Pancake Filling: In a sizable bowl, incorporate one large clove clove garlic, 1/4 teaspoon salt, 3 tablespoons soy sauce, 1 tablespoon rice wine vinegar, 1/2 teaspoon sesame oil, and 1/2 teaspoon chili flakes and whisk to mix. Add 2 ounces bean sprouts, 1/2 pound carrots, 1/2 pound seeded and julienned english cucumber, 2-3 3 scallions cut into narrow ribbons, 1 teaspoon salt, and 1/2 teaspoon sugar. Combine well and let sit for just two hours.

Warm pancakes, spread Hoisen sauce on pancake, fill with vegetables and roll.

Presentation: Place pork loin on a plate. Garnish with two filled, rolled, warmed mushu pancakes. Garnish with fresh cilantro.

Garnish Option: Make a reduced amount of duck stock, star anise, and plum wine. Reduce to glaze and lightly puddle on plate before adding pork chop and mushu pancakes

Early Autumn Smoked Pork Chops

Ingredients:

   1 cup ketchup
   1 cup soy sauce
   1/2 cup white sugar
   1/4 cup strawberry jelly
   2 tablespoons prepared horseradish
   2 tablespoons tomato paste
   1 tablespoon butter
   1 tablespoon vegetable oil
   1 tablespoon vinegar
   1/2 teaspoon salt
   1/2 teaspoon ground black pepper
   1 pinch ground paprika
   1 1/2 pounds bone-in pork chops

Directions:

Step one 1 Combine ketchup, soy sauce, sugar, strawberry jelly, horseradish, tomato paste, butter, oil, vinegar, salt, black pepper, and paprika together in a saucepan over low heat; cook and stir until marinade is smooth, about five minutes.

Step two 2 Place pork chops in a bowl; add marinade. Marinate pork chops in the refrigerator for one hour.

Step three 3 Remove pork chops from marinade, reserving the excess marinade.

Step 4 Light charcoals in the grill and add several bags of fall leaves throughout obtaining the coals ready for grilling.

Step 5 Place pork chops on the grill when the coals are about halfway ashed over. Baste pork chops with marinade and flip pork chops. Cover grill with lid so smoke from the leaves can permeate the pork chops. Cook until pork is slightly pink in the guts, 20 to thirty minutes. An instant-read thermometer inserted in to the center should read at least 145 degrees F (63 degrees C).

Easy Grilled Pork Chops

Ingredients:

1/4 cup honey
2 tablespoons vegetable oil
1 tablespoon apple cider vinegar
1 teaspoon ground cumin
1/2 teaspoon red pepper flakes
eight 1/2-inch bone-in pork chops (about 3 ounces each)
salt and freshly ground black pepper

Directions:

Start by making the marinade. In a tiny bowl, whisk together the honey, oil, vinegar, cumin and red pepper flakes. Easy, right?

Sprinkle both sides of the pork chops with salt and pepper and place in a re-sealable plastic bag with the marinade. Let rest on the counter for one hour. That's easy.

Heat a grill or grill pan over medium heat. Take away the pork chops from the bag and lightly sprinkle with salt and pepper. Put on the grill and cook before pork chop releases from the grill, about 4 minutes. Flip and cook on the other hand for another three minutes. If by using a grill pan, make certain to accomplish in batches which means you don't steam the chops. And do not worry should you have neither; you can certainly do this in a pan. See, easy!

Emeril's Shake 'Em Up Pork Chops

Ingredients:

1/2 cup dry white wine
1/4 cup plus 1/3 cup olive oil
2 teaspoons liquid concentrate crab and shrimp boil (recommended: zatarain's)
2 teaspoons liquid concentrate crab and shrimp boil (recommended: zatarain's)
1/2 teaspoon ground black pepper
1/2 teaspoon cayenne pepper
3 cloves garlic , smashed
1 bay leaf
4 bone-in center-cut pork loin chops, about 12 ounces each
1 cup dry bread crumbs
1/2 cup masa harina
1 1/2 cups finely grated parmesan
1 tablespoon essence, recipe follows
1/3 cup olive oil
cheesy potatoes au gratin, recipe follows
grilled asparagus, for serving
2 1/2 tablespoons paprika
2 tablespoons salt
2 tablespoons garlic powder
1 tablespoon black pepper
1 tablespoon onion powder
1 tablespoon cayenne pepper
1 tablespoon dried oregano

1 tablespoon dried thyme
2 pounds idaho potatoes , peeled and thinly sliced
salt
freshly ground black pepper
8 ounces cheddar, grated
1 1/2 cups heavy cream

Directions:

In an enormous resealable plastic bag, incorporate your wine, 1/4 cup of the oil, the crab boil, pepper, cayenne, garlic, and bay leaf. Add the pork chops and marinate, refrigerated, turning occasionally, for 2 to 4 hours.

In a clean, large plastic bag, incorporate the bread crumbs, masa harina, Parmesan, and Essence. Shake to mix.

Get rid of the pork chops from the marinade and shake to eradicate any excess. Individually, add the chops to the dry mixture and shake until evenly coated. Remove, placed on an enormous plate, and refrigerate for quarter-hour.

In an enormous skillet or saute pan, heat all of those other 1/3 cup of oil over medium-high heat. Add the chops and cook until golden brown and cooked through, 5 to 6 minutes per side.

Remove from the pan and serve immediately along with portions of the Cheesy Potatoes au Gratin, with grilled asparagus privately.

Combine all Ingredients: thoroughly. Recipe from "New New Orleans Cooking", by Emeril Lagasse and Jessie Tirsch, published by William and Morrow, 1993.

Preheat the oven to 400 degrees F. Lightly grease a medium gratin dish with butter.

Cover underneath of the pan with an overlapping layer of potatoes. Lightly season with salt and pepper and top with a sprinkling of cheese (about 2 tablespoons). Continue layering potatoes, seasoning, and cheese, ending with all of those other cheese at the very top. Pour the cream over the potatoes, pressing lightly using your hands to cover the potatoes with cream. Cover with aluminum foil and bake before cheese is absorbed into the potatoes and the potatoes are tender when pierced with a knife, about 50 minutes. Get rid of the foil and bake before mixture is bubbly and the most effective is golden brown, about 10 minutes.

Remove from the oven and let rest 10 minutes before cutting into portions.

Fabienne's Grilled Center Cut Pork Chops Recipe

Ingredients:

2 tablespoons mayonnaise
2 tablespoons marsala wine
1 tablespoon dried basil
1 tablespoon paprika
1 teaspoon garlic powder
1 teaspoon worcestershire sauce
1 teaspoon lemon juice
1/2 teaspoon celery salt
teaspoon ? cayenne pepper
2 eaches center-cut boneless pork chops

Directions:

Step one 1 Whisk mayonnaise, Marsala wine, basil, paprika, garlic powder, Worcestershire sauce, lemon juice, celery salt, and cayenne pepper together in a bowl and pour right into a resealable plastic bag. Add pork chops, coat with the marinade, squeeze out excess air, and seal the bag. Marinate in the refrigerator for 8 hours to overnight.

Step two 2 Preheat grill to 400 degrees F (200 degrees C) and lightly oil the grates.

Step 3 3 Take away the pork chops from marinade and shake to eliminate excess moisture.

Step 4 Cook pork chops on the preheated grill, basting with marinade every a quarter-hour, until an instant-read thermometer reads 165 degrees F (74 degrees C), 30 to 40 minutes.

Filipino Grilled Pork Chops

Ingredients:

3/4 cup apple cider vinegar
2 tablespoons soy sauce
1 tablespoon fish sauce
1/4 cup sugar
1/2 teaspoon red pepper flakes
3 cloves garlic , finely chopped
4 bone-in pork blade chops (1/2 inch thick; 6 to 7 ounces each)
1 lemon, halved
2 bunches scallions, trimmed
2 tablespoons vegetable oil , plus more for the grill
kosher salt and freshly ground pepper
1 cup jasmine rice

Directions:

Combine the vinegar, soy sauce, fish sauce, sugar, red pepper flakes and garlic in a medium bowl and stir before sugar is dissolved. Transfer 1/4 cup sauce to a tiny bowl and reserve for serving.

Combine the pork chops and remaining sauce in a 1-gallon zip-top bag. Squeeze in the lemon juice and add the squeezed lemon halves; seal the bag. Let marinate

20 minutes at room temperature, massaging the pork every five minutes. Toss the scallions with the vegetable oil on a plate and season with salt and pepper.

Meanwhile, cook the rice as the label directs. Preheat a grill or grill pan to medium high. Take away the pork chops from the marinade, pat dry and season with salt and pepper. Oil the grill or grill pan, add the pork and grill until just cooked through, three to four 4 minutes per side. Transfer to a plate to rest. Grill the scallions, turning, until marked and wilted, one to two 2 minutes. Divide the rice, scallions and pork chops among plates. Serve with the reserved sauce.

Fontina and Prosciutto Stuffed Pork Chops with Grilled Polenta Squares and Roasted California Grapes

Ingredients:

4 bone-in pork chops , about 1 1/2 inches thick
2 quarts water
1/4 cup sugar
1/4 cup kosher salt
4 fresh thyme sprigs
10 cloves
6 allspice berries
8 slices (about 3 ounces) prosciutto
4 slices (about 3 ounces) fontina
1/2 cup chicken stock
4 tablespoons unsalted butter, chilled
4 sprigs flat-leaf parsley, for garnish
1 pound california red grapes, on the vine and cut into 4 smaller clusters/bunches
extra-virgin olive oil
kosher salt and freshly ground black pepper
grilled polenta squares, recipe follows
8 cups water
1 teaspoon kosher salt
2 cups polenta/yellow cornmeal
1/4 cup heavy cream
2 tablespoons unsalted butter, room temperature

1 cup grated parmigiano-reggiano
fresh cracked black pepper
extra-virgin olive oil

Directions:

Prepare the pork chops. Make a brine by combining the water, sugar, salt, thyme sprigs, clove and all-spice berries in a re-sealable bag. Add the pork chops, seal up the bag and devote the refrigerator for approximately 30 minutes.

Preheat oven to 425 degrees F.

Drain the pork chops and pat dry. Utilizing a paring knife, make a horizontal cut in to the center of each chop to generate a pocket. Stuff a slice of fontina and prosciutto inside each pocket and secure with a toothpick. Set 2 large cast iron skillets over medium-high heat and put in a 2-count of extra-virgin essential olive oil to each skillet. Add 2 chops to each one of the skillets and cook for 4 to five minutes until golden. Turn chops, push to at least one 1 side and set grape clusters in pan. Drizzle with just a little essential olive oil and season with salt and pepper before putting the pans in the oven. Roast chops for 5 to 7 minutes until cooked through and cheese has melted. Remove from oven when done and set chops and clusters of roasted grapes aside on a plate - keep warm.

Consolidate juices into 1 pan and set over medium heat. Put in a splash of chicken stock to the pan, scraping underneath to extract all of the flavors. Fold in cold butter while whisking to thicken sauce. Season with salt and pepper. To serve, set 1 pork chop on each plate along with a Grilled Polenta Square, garnish with a cluster of roasted grapes and drizzle with pan sauce. Set a collection of hydroponic watercress to at least one 1 side and serve.

Bring water and salt to a boil in a big saucepan. Gradually whisk in the cornmeal in a slow steady stream. Lower heat and continue steadily to whisk before polenta is thick and smooth, about 20 minutes. Add the cream and butter and continue steadily to stir until incorporated. Remove from heat; fold in Parmesan and black pepper. Pour the polenta right into a buttered 9 by 13-inch shallow baking dish and spread evenly with a spatula. Cover and chill a couple of hours. Slice the polenta into squares. Brush both sides with essential olive oil and transfer to a hot grill. Grill on both sides until golden brown.

Glazed Grilled Pork Chops Recipe

Ingredients:

2 tablespoons dark brown sugar, or to taste
1 cup ketchup
1 cup mayonnaise
1/2 cup prepared yellow mustard
1/4 cup worcestershire sauce
1 teaspoon chili powder
teaspoon ? ground cayenne pepper
6 raw chop with refuse, 185 g; (blank) 6.5 ounces (3/4 inch thick) pork chops

Directions:

The first step 1 1 Preheat a patio patio grill for medium-high heat, and lightly oil the grate.

Second step two 2 Place the brown sugar, ketchup, mayonnaise, yellow mustard, Worcestershire sauce, chili powder, and cayenne pepper directly into a bowl, and stir until blended.

Third step three 3 Place the pork chops on the preheated grill, and cook the chops before surface is seared on the other hand the meat is merely barely pink in the centre, about five minutes. Brush the chops with the glaze mixture, and flip to cook the glaze onto the meat. When the glazed side shows good grill marks, flip again, brush glaze onto the pork chops, flip, and grill before other side shows nice brown grill marks. An instant-read thermometer inserted in to the center of a chop should read 145 degrees F (63 degrees C).

Grilled 'Fusion' Pork Chops Recipe

Ingredients:

- 1/4 cup soy sauce
- 1/4 cup lime juice
- 1 tablespoon garlic paste
- 1 tablespoon ginger paste
- 4 eaches (1-inch-thick) pork chops
- 1 tablespoon garam masala

Directions:

The first step 1 In a bowl, stir together soy sauce, lime juice, garlic, and ginger. .

Second step 2 Place pork chops in a glass dish. Pour soy sauce mixture over chops. Cover, and refrigerate 2-3 3 hours, turning occasionally.

Step three 3 3 Preheat an outdoor patio grill for direct heat and lightly oil grate.

Step 4 Place chops on the grill. Because they cook, sprinkle with garam masala. Cook about 10 minutes on each side.

Grilled Apple Brined Pork Chops

Ingredients:

2 cups apple juice apple juice
1 tablespoon black pepper coarsely ground black pepper
1/4 cup salt salt
1/4 cup light brown sugar light brown sugar
1 teaspoon red pepper flakes red pepper flakes
5 ribs pork chops end pork chops about 1 1/2 pounds
1 tablespoon seasoning grill seasoning

Directions:

In a huge pot over medium-high heat, add 1 cup of water, juice , pepper, salt, sugar and red pepper flakes. recreate a simmer ensuring to stir occasionally to dissolve the salt and sugar. Remove from heat and increase an outsized bowl with 2 cups of ice.

After the brined has cooled add pork chops. Brine for at the least 4 hours or up to a day within the refrigerator.

Remove pork from brine, rinse with cool water and pat dry with paper towels.

Heat grill or grill pan over medium heat. Sprinkle 1 side of the pork chops with 1/2 the grill seasoning. Place chops on hot oiled grill, seasoned side down. Sprinkle the topside with remaining grill seasoning. Grill chops for 4 to 5 minutes per side. Let rest for 5 minutes before serving.

Grilled Asian Ginger Pork Chops

Ingredients:

1/2 cup orange juice
2 tablespoons soy sauce
2 tablespoons minced fresh ginger root
2 tablespoons grated orange zest
1 teaspoon minced garlic
1 teaspoon garlic chile paste
1/2 teaspoon salt
6 pork loin chops, 1/2 inch thick

Directions:

In a shallow container, mix together juice, soy sauce, ginger, orange peel, garlic, chile paste, and salt. Add pork chops, and switch to coat evenly. Cover, and refrigerate for at the least 2 hours, or overnight. Turn the pork chops within the marinade occasionally.

Preheat grill for top level heat, and lightly oil grate.

Grill pork chops for five to six minutes per side, or even to desired doneness.

Grilled Berkshire Pork Chop with Merlot Sauce

Ingredients:

2 medium sweet potatoes, peeled and chopped
2 tablespoons butter
1/4 cup maple syrup
3 cups beef broth
1 cup merlot wine
1 tablespoon cornstarch
1/4 cup water
kosher salt and freshly ground black pepper
4 (4-ounce) pork chops
kosher salt and freshly ground black pepper
2 tablespoons olive oil

Directions:

To cook the sweet potatoes: Place them in a medium saucepot and cover with water. Bring the water to a simmer over medium heat. Cook before potatoes are tender, about 20 minutes. Drain the potatoes and place them straight into a food processor. Add the butter and maple syrup and process until smooth and creamy. (The sweet potatoes may be mashed yourself.)
Transfer to a bowl and keep warm or cool and reheat.

To make the sauce: Combine the broth and wine in a saucepan. Bring to a simmer over medium heat then reduce by one third1 / 3. Meanwhile, in simply a little bowl whisk the cornstarch with 1/4 cup water until smooth. Whisk the cornstarch mixture into the simmering sauce. Continue whisking before sauce thickens. Season with salt and pepper and keep warm over low heat.

To cook the pork: Heat a cast iron skillet or grill pan over temperature. Season the pork with salt and pepper. Brush the chops with oil then cook until barely pink at the guts, about 4 minutes per side. Allow pork to rest for 5 minutes. Arrange sweet potatoes and pork chops on 2 plates. Spoon sauce around the chops and serve.

Grilled Bone-In Pork Chops

Ingredients:

2 to 3 rosemary sprigs, stems removed and leaves coarsely chopped
kosher salt and freshly ground pepper
1 granny smith or other crisp apple , cored and seeded
2 center-cut bone-in pork chops (about 3/4-inch thick)
4 tablespoons extra-virgin olive oil

Directions:

Make a grill for high temperature. Whisk together the oil, rosemary and a pinch each of salt and pepper.

Cut the apple horizontally into 1/4-inch-thick slices; brush the slices with the oil mixture and grill, covered, until grill marks appear about 1 minute per side.

Brush the chops with the oil mixture and grill, covered, for 1 minute; rotate the chops a half-turn without flipping, and grill, covered, for 1 minute more. Flip the chops and grill, covered, 1 minute; rotate and grill, covered, 1 minute more. Transfer the chops to a plate, cover with foil and let rest for five minutes before serving with the apple slices as garnish.

Grilled Bone-in Pork Chops with Hawaiian Marinade

Ingredients:

4 bone-in pork loin chops, cut 3/4-in. thick
2 cans (6 oz. each) unsweetened pineapple juice (1 1/2 c.)
3 scallions, white parts sliced into thin rounds
3 tablespoons peeled and minced ginger
3 tablespoons reduced-sodium soy sauce
2 tablespoons asian dark sesame oil
2 tablespoons light brown sugar
3/4 teaspoon freshly ground black pepper
1/2 teaspoon coarse salt

Directions:

Mix pineapple juice, white factors of scallions, ginger, soy sauce, sesame oil, brown sugar, pepper and salt in large, resealable bag. Add chops, seal bag and refrigerate for 2 to 10 hr. Remove chops from marinade and pat off excess marinade with paper towels. Discard remaining marinade.

Make a medium-hot fire in grill. Brush grill grate clean and lightly oil grate. Grill chops directly over heat, 8 to 10 min., turning once, until internal temperature on a thermometer reads 145 degrees F, along with a 3-min. rest.

Grilled Brown Sugar Pork Chops

Ingredients:

1/2 cup brown sugar, firmly packed
1/2 cup apple juice
4 tablespoons vegetable oil
1 tablespoon soy sauce
1/2 teaspoon ground ginger
salt and pepper to taste
2 teaspoons cornstarch
1/2 cup water
6 raw chop with refuse, 113 g; (blank) 4 ounces boneless pork chops

Directions:

Step one 1 Preheat a patio grill for high temperature.

Step two 2 In a tiny saucepan, incorporate brown sugar, apple juice, oil, soy sauce, ginger, salt, and pepper. Bring to boil. Combine water and cornstarch in normal size bowl, and whisk into brown sugar mixture. Stir until thick.

Step three 3 Brush grate lightly with oil before positioning pork chops on the grill. Cook over hot coals for 10 to 12 minutes, turning once. Brush with sauce right before removing chops from grill. Serve with remaining sauce.

Grilled Corn Salad with Lime, Red Chili and Cotija

Ingredients:

8 ears fresh corn, silks removed, husk on, soaked in cold water 30 minutes
canola oil
salt and freshly ground black pepper
1/4 cup creme fraiche
2 limes, juiced and 1 zested
1 tablespoon ancho chili powder
1/4 cup chopped fresh cilantro leaves
1/4 cup grated cotija cheese

Directions:

Heat grill to high. Grill corn until charred on all sides, 10 roughly minutes. Remove the grill and take away the kernels with a sharp knife. When you are cutting the corn, put a cast iron skillet on the grill to heat.

Add the corn and the rest of the Ingredients: to the hot pan and cook, stirring occasionally, until creamy and heated through. Serve with the steak.

Grilled Giant Pork Chops with Sweet Peach Barbecue Sauce

Ingredients:

3 tablespoons ground coriander
3 tablespoons ground paprika
2 tablespoons ground cumin
1 tablespoon kosher salt
3 tablespoons freshly ground black pepper
1 tablespoon brown sugar
4 ribs or loin pork chops , about 1 1/2-inch thick (12 to 14 ounces each)
2 tablespoons olive oil
1 small red onion , peeled, sliced thin
3 peaches , pitted, cut into medium sized cubes
2 tablespoons peeled and minced fresh ginger
2 medium ripe tomatoes , cut into medium sized cubes
1/2 cup cider vinegar
1/2 cup orange juice
1/3 cup light or dark brown sugar
1 teaspoon ground allspice
salt and freshly ground black pepper

Directions:

Create a multi-level fire in the grill: Leave 1/4 of underneath clear of coals, bank the coals in all of those other 3/4 of the grill so that they are 3 x as along with 1 side as on the other. When the coals are ignited and the temperature has lowered to medium (hold hand about 5-inches above grill grid, over the spot where coals are deepest, for 4 to 5 seconds), the grill is getting ready to cook.

Make spice rub: Combine the Ingredients for the spice rub in a little bowl and mix well. Rub the pork chops generously on both sides with the mixture and reserve while making the sauce.

Make the sauce: In an enormous skillet over medium-high heat, heat the oil until hot, however, not smoking. Add the onions and cook, stirring occasionally, until golden brown, about 11 to 13 minutes. Add the peaches, ginger, and tomatoes and cook, stirring frequently for 2 minutes. Stir in the vinegar, orange juice, sugar, allspice, and salt and pepper, to taste. Bring the mixture to a boil, then reduce the heat and simmer before mixture is reduced by about 1/2 and thickened slightly, about 20 minutes. Taste and modify for the seasoning, then transfer the sauce to a blender or food processor and puree until smooth (be mindful with hot liquids). Reserve 1/4 cup sauce for basting the chops, then pour all of those other sauce right into a tiny serving bowl.

Put the chops on the grill over the coals and cook, turning once, until desired doneness; 8 to 10 minutes per side for medium. During the last 30 seconds of cooking on each side, baste the chops generously with the sauce. Search for doneness.

Serve the chops hot with extra barbecue sauce privately.

Cook's note: The spice rub and barbecue sauce contains sugar, that may burn while cooking on the grill. If the chops figure out how to burn externally, move them to cooler part of the grill and cover with a metal pie pan or disposable foil to complete cooking.

Grilled Hoisin Pork Chop Noodle Bowl

Ingredients:

2 tablespoons hoisin sauce
8 ounces boneless pork loin chops, (two to three 1/2-inch-thick chops)
kosher salt and freshly ground black pepper
8 ounces thin rice noodles
1 japanese eggplant , sliced 1/2-inch thick on the bias
4 ounces string beans , stem ends trimmed
2 tablespoons vegetable oil
1/4 cup fish sauce
2 tablespoons light brown sugar
4 teaspoons rice vinegar
1 teaspoon chili-garlic sauce , plus more for serving
1 cup lightly packed fresh cilantro leaves
1 cup cherry tomatoes , halved
1/4 cup chopped roasted peanuts

Directions:

Heat a grill pan over medium-high heat.

Brush the hoisin sauce on both sides of every pork chop, and sprinkle both sides lightly with salt and pepper. Rest at room temperature for a quarter-hour.

Bring 12 cups water to a boil in a sizable saucepan. Remove from heat and add the dried rice noodles to submerge. When the noodles are tender but nonetheless involve some bite, about three minutes, drain through an excellent mesh sieve. Reserve the noodles for a later use.

Toss the eggplant and string beans in the oil with some salt and pepper, and transfer to the grill. Cook the eggplant until tender nonetheless they still hold their shape, 2-3 three minutes per side. Grill the string beans, turning occasionally, until charred and crisp-tender, about 4 minutes. Transfer the eggplant and string beans to a cutting board and cut into bite-size pieces.

Decrease the heat to medium. Grill the pork chops until just cooked through, 2 minutes per side. Take away the pork chops to a plate and rest for five minutes, then thinly slice over the grain.

In a tiny bowl, mix together the fish sauce, sugar, vinegar, chili-garlic sauce and 1/2 cup water.

Divide the noodles, pork slices, eggplant, string beans, cilantro, tomatoes, peanuts and fish sauce mixture among four large serving bowls. Serve with an increase of chili-garlic sauce privately.

Grilled Italian Pork Chops

Ingredients:

4 eaches (3/4 inch thick) pork chops
1 pinch salt and ground black pepper to taste
4 slices ham
4 slices tomato
4 slices mozzarella cheese
1 teaspoon chopped fresh oregano to taste
1 pinch paprika to taste

Directions:

Step one 1 Preheat a patio grill for medium heat, and lightly oil the grate. .

Step two 2 Sprinkle pork chops with salt and black pepper, and grill before chops are browned, show good grill marks, and so are no longer pink in the centre, 5 to 8 minutes per side. An instant-read meat thermometer inserted in to the center of a chop should read at least 145 degrees F (63 degrees C).

Step three 3 Place ham, tomato, and mozzarella cheese slices on each pork chop, and sprinkle with oregano and paprika; cook before cheese has melted, about 2 more minutes. Let are a symbol of five minutes before serving.

Grilled Jamaican Jerked Pork Loin Chops

Ingredients:

1/2 (12-ounce) bottle lager style beer
3 fluid ounces dark rum
1/4 cup molasses
1/4 cup soy sauce
1/4 cup lime juice
2 tablespoons minced garlic
2 tablespoons minced ginger
1 scotch bonnet chile pepper, minced
2 teaspoons chopped fresh thyme
2 teaspoons chopped fresh marjoram
1 1/2 teaspoons ground allspice
2 teaspoons ground cinnamon
1 teaspoon ground nutmeg
2 leaves (blank)s bay leaves
8 (6 ounce) pork loin chops
1/2 teaspoon kosher salt and cracked black pepper to taste

Directions:

Step one 1 Pour the beer, rum, molasses, soy sauce, and lime juice right into a bowl. Stir in the garlic, ginger, scotch bonnet pepper, thyme, and marjoram. Season with allspice, cinnamon, nutmeg, and bay leaves. Place the pork chops right into a zip top bag, and pour in the marinade. Refrigerate overnight.

Step two 2 Prepare a patio grill for medium heat. Take the pork chops out of your marinade, put on a plate, and invite to sit at room temperature for 15 to 20 minutes as the grill heats.

Step three 3 Season the chops to taste with kosher salt and cracked black pepper. Grill the chops on both sides until a thermometer inserted in to the center registers 145 degrees F (63 degrees C). Permit the pork chops to rest for approximately five minutes before serving to permit the juices to redistribute.

Grilled Korean-Style BBQ Glazed Pork Chops with Red Onions and Baby Bok Choy

Ingredients:

2 tablespoons soy sauce
1 tablespoon chili garlic sauce , such as sriracha
1 tablespoon toasted sesame oil
1 tablespoon light brown sugar
1 tablespoon rice vinegar
1 tablespoon peeled and finely grated fresh ginger
1 clove garlic , grated
1/2 cup hoisin sauce
4 bone-in pork chops (about 3 pounds)
kosher salt and freshly ground black pepper
kosher salt and freshly ground black pepper
1 red onion , cut into 1/2-inch-thick slices
4 to 6 baby bok choy, halved lengthwise (about 1 pound)

Directions:

Preheat a grill to medium-high heat. Stir together the soy sauce, chili sauce, sesame oil, brown sugar, vinegar, grated ginger and grated garlic in a little bowl. Reserve 2 tablespoons for the vegetables and stir in the hoisin sauce. Set half aside for serving with the cooked pork chops and stir in a single to two 2 tablespoons water.

Sprinkle the pork chops on both sides with 1/2 teaspoon each salt and pepper for all 4 chops. Place the pork chops and onions on a lightly oiled grill. Grill before pork chops are simply just slightly pink near the bone, 6 minutes on the first side and 4 to 5 minutes on another side. Grill the onions until they are soft. Start brushing both pork and the onions with the hoisin sauce mixture about halfway through grilling. Transfer the pork chops to a cutting board to rest for about 5 minutes and the onions to a bowl. Put the bok choy in a big bowl and cover with plastic wrap. Microwave before center core has softened and could easily be pierced with the finish of a sharp knife, 3 to 5 5 minutes. Season the bok choy with 1/4 teaspoon each salt and pepper and grill until charred, 2-3 3 minutes per side. Improve the bowl with the onions and gently toss with the reserved 2 tablespoons ginger sauce. Serve the pork chops with the grilled vegetables and the reserved hoisin sauce mixture privately.

Grilled Lemon Herb Pork Chops

Ingredients:

1/4 cup lemon juice
2 tablespoons vegetable oil
4 cloves garlic , minced
1 teaspoon salt
1/4 teaspoon dried oregano
1/4 teaspoon pepper
6 (4 ounce) boneless pork loin chops

Directions:

Step one 1 In a huge resealable bag, incorporate lemon juice, oil, garlic, salt, oregano, and pepper. Place chops in bag, seal, and refrigerate 2 hours or overnight. Turn bag frequently to distribute marinade. .

Step two 2 Preheat a patio grill for high temperature. Remove chops from bag, and transfer remaining marinade to a saucepan. Bring marinade to a boil, remove from heat, and reserve.

Step three 3 Lightly oil the grill grate. Grill pork chops for 5 to 7 minutes per side, basting frequently with boiled marinade, until done.

Grilled Mongolian Pork Chops Recipe

Ingredients:

1/2 cup hoisin sauce
4 cloves garlic , minced
1 1/2 tablespoons soy sauce
1 tablespoon grated fresh ginger
1 tablespoon red wine vinegar
1 tablespoon rice vinegar
1 tablespoon sherry vinegar
2 teaspoons sesame oil
2 teaspoons white sugar
1 1/2 teaspoons hot sauce
1/2 teaspoon ground white peppers
1/2 teaspoon freshly ground black pepper
2 (10 ounce) thick bone-in center cut pork chops
1/4 cup red wine vinegar
3 tablespoons white sugar
2 tablespoons hot mustard powder to taste
1 egg yolk
1/3 cup creme fraiche
1 teaspoon dijon mustard
1/4 teaspoon ground turmeric
cayenne pepper to taste

Directions:

Combine hoisin sauce, garlic, soy sauce, ginger, 1 tablespoon burgandy or merlot wine vinegar, rice vinegar, sherry vinegar, sesame oil, 2 teaspoons sugar, hot sauce, white pepper, and black pepper in an enormous bowl. Whisk thoroughly and reserve.

Place pork chops in a resealable freezer bag; pour slightly far more than 1/2 the marinade into freezer bag over pork chops. Seal bag and refrigerate for 6 to 8 8 hours. Reserve remaining marinade.

Combine 1/4 cup burgandy or merlot wine vinegar, 3 tablespoons sugar, 2 tablespoons hot mustard powder, and egg yolk in a little saucepan over medium-low heat. Whisk until slightly thickened, about 5 minutes; remove from heat. Stir in creme fraiche, Dijon mustard, turmeric, and cayenne pepper. Refrigerate until needed.

Remove pork chops from marinade and pat dry using paper towel.

Preheat an outdoor patio grill for temperature, and lightly oil the grate.

Cook pork chops on the preheated grill until browned grill marks appear, about 4 minutes per side.

Move pork chops from directly above heat source. Continue cooking over indirect medium heat, brushing all of those other marinade on each side, until forget about pink inside, about 25 minutes. An instant-read thermometer inserted into the center should read 145 degrees F (63 degrees C). Serve pork chops topped with mustard sauce.

Honey Mustard BBQ Pork Chops Recipe

Ingredients

1/3 cup honey
3 tablespoons orange juice
1 tablespoon apple cider vinegar
1 teaspoon white wine
1 teaspoon worcestershire sauce
2 teaspoons onion powder , or to taste
1/4 teaspoon dried tarragon
3 tablespoons dijon mustard
8 raw chop with refuse, 106 g; yields excluding refuses thin cut pork chops

Directions

Step 1 Place honey, fruit juice, vinegar, wine, Worcester sauce , onion powder, tarragon, and mustard during a large resealable bag . Slash fatty fringe of each chop in about three places without cutting into the meat; this may prevent the meat from curling during cooking. Place chops within the bag, and marinate within the refrigerator for a minimum of 2 hours.

Step 2 Preheat grill for top heat.

Step 3 Lightly oil grill grate. Place chops on grill, and discard marinade. Cook chops for six to eight minutes, turning once, or to desired doneness.

Honey Mustard Dream Delight Pork Chops

Ingredients

1/4 cup ground black pepper
4 tablespoons ground cayenne pepper
4 tablespoons garlic powder
2 tablespoons paprika
1/4 cup packed brown sugar
2 tablespoons chili powder
6 raw chop with refuse, 106 g; yields excluding refuses pork chops
4 tablespoons prepared mustard
4 tablespoons prepared horseradish mustard
1/4 cup prepared brown mustard
2 teaspoons prepared horseradish
1/4 cup packed brown sugar
4 tablespoons honey

Directions

Step 1 during a small bowl, combine the bottom black pepper, cayenne pepper, garlic powder, paprika, sugar and flavorer . Mix well and rub thoroughly over the pork chops. Cover the meat and refrigerate for twenty-four hours, taking meat out a minimum of 30 to 45 minutes before grilling.

Step 2 Prepare an outside grill for top heat and lightly oil grate.

Step 3 Meanwhile, during a small bowl, combine the yellow mustard, horseradish mustard, brown mustard, horseradish and sugar. Mix well. Place the honey during a separate small bowl.

Step 4 Then, still grill over medium high heat, turning and basting every 10 minutes with the sauce, for 45 to 50 minutes, or until internal temperature reaches 145 degrees F (63 degrees C). During the last quarter-hour of cooking, start basting with the honey, turning as required. this may give the chops a pleasant, sweet coating, sealing within the flavors of the mustard baste.

Part 2

Classic/Boring Grilled Cheese

2 slices white bread
1/3 cup grated cheddar cheese
Garlic dill pickles, on the side

This is a boring recipe but kids will like it. Don't use too much cheese or it won't melt. (This applies to most things in life, especially the recipes in this book.)

Tomato and Basil Grilled Cheese

2 slices white bread
1/3 cup grated cheddar cheese
1 medium tomato, sliced
1 teaspoon dried basil

Feed this to Italian people and they will love you. Fresh basil works as well. Be generous like it's Christmas.

Tomato and Bacon

2 slices white bread
1/3 cup grated cheddar cheese
1 medium tomato, sliced
3 slices bacon, crisp

Don't cheap out on the bacon. Thick is good. Smoked with apple wood is the best. Ask your butcher, he'll back me up on this. If he doesn't, find a new butcher.

Leftover Jalapeno

2 slices white bread
1/3 cup grated cheddar cheese
Leftover fresh jalapeno, or leftover canned stuff
1/4 cup crushed nacho chips

You ever make nachos and have some jalapeno pepper leftover? Now you know what to do with it. You make a grilled cheese that'll knock your socks off.
The crushed nachos give it a (spoiler alert) nice crunchy taste.
Funny story: I served this to my brother once and he didn't like it. I forget he couldn't handle spicy things.

Grilled Cheese Fingers

2 slices white bread
1/3 cup grated cheddar cheese
Olives, on the side

When you finish cooking the grilled cheese, slice it into strips. If you want to get fancy you can put each strip back into the pan and fry the edges for a few seconds.

The Creamy Red Goat

2 slices white bread
1/4 cup grated cheddar cheese
1/4 cup cream cheese
1/4 cup sweet pickled red peppers, chopped

Stir the goat cheese into the cream cheese before you fry it. Say a prayer to the Lord of Goats.

Spicy Mayo Thing

2 slices white bread
1/3 cup grated Monterey Jack cheese
5 hot pepper rings
2 tablespoons mayonnaise

Spread the mayonnaise outside the sandwich if you're feeling adventurous. I was at a diner where they did it like that once. It was strange but enjoyable, like when you take your wife to Mexico and she says: "Let's bring another couple back to our room and see what happens." Months later your marriage is on the rocks because now she's really into swinging but for you it was just okay. You're a meat and potatoes guy but she wants the all-you-can-eat Asian fusion buffet.

Sriracha Mayo Grilled Cheese

2 slices white bread
1/3 cup grated cheddar cheese
1 tablespoon mayonnaise
1 tablespoon Sriracha hot sauce

Combine the Sriracha hot sauce with the mayonnaise and stir with a miniature spoon until combined or you get dizzy. Thank whatever dwarf you stole the spoon from.
You could also just 2 tablespoons of Sriracha mayonnaise if you live somewhere it's readily available. Sorry, Canada.

Pesto Tomato

2 slices white bread
1 tablespoon pesto
1 medium tomato, sliced
1 slice American cheese
1 slice provolone cheese

I recommend wedging the pesto and the tomato between both slices of cheese forming a sort of secondary sandwich. Trust me this is the best way to do it. I wouldn't lie to you now that I've got your money.

Havarti and Seafood Salad

2 slices white bread
2 slices Havarti cheese
3 tablespoons Seafood salad

I came upon this recipe while visiting my dying aunt in Newfoundland. She told me she had left me something priceless in her will. Something I would cherish forever. It was money. I got the recipe from a diner called Fat Joey's.

Garlic Bread and Cheese

2 slices garlic bread from the grocery store, you know, that stuff that comes in an aluminum-looking silver bag you reheat in the oven.
1/3 cup grated cheddar cheese
5 meatballs, from your own homemade spaghetti and meatballs (you can't have my recipe)

I was dating this chick whose favorite meal was store-bought garlic bread and homemade spaghetti and meatballs. We always made too much and some had leftover in the morning. I turned it into grilled cheese. Two months later we broke up. She's married now with two kids and some kind of rat-dog terrier.

Guacamole and Stuff

2 slices white bread
1/3 cup grated leftover cheese you bought for nachos
2 tablespoons guacamole

You know those bags of pre-grated cheese you see at the grocery store but never buy unless they're on sale and even when you do buy them there's way too much in the bag even after you make four plates of nachos? That's the cheese you want to use for this recipe. Any other type of cheese would be a disaster.

Movie Popcorn Grilled Cheese

2 slices white bread
1/3 cup grated cheddar cheese
1/2 cup movie-style popcorn

If it's not movie-style it won't have enough butter in it to taste great. Don't put that air-blown junk your mother eats as a snack after her fitness group into your grilled cheese. It will taste like crap and you'll regret every decision you ever made. Serve with nacho cheese sauce if possible.

Mushrooms and Swiss Cheese

2 slices white bread
6 white mushrooms, chopped
1 small onion, diced
2 cloves garlic, minced
2 slices Swiss cheese
1 tablespoon olive oil

Sauté the mushrooms, garlic, and onion in the olive oil. You know the rest. Serve this sandwich to somebody you want to sleep with and make up a fancy name for it. You should probably also lie about how much money you make.

Rabbi's Delight

2 slices white bread
2 slices, Montreal smoked meat
1 tablespoon spicy mustard
1/4 cup cream cheese

Serve this to your friends who know to spell *synagogue*.

Cajun Shrimp

6 cooked shrimp, stemmed or whatever you call it
1/4 teaspoon Cajun seasoning
1/3 cup grated cheddar cheese
2 slices white bread

Taylor Kitsch was alright as Gambit, but he totally killed it in *True Detective* Season 2, which most people thought was garbage but after I watched it a second time I decided it was alright.

Roasted Tomatoes

4 plum tomatoes
salt, pepper, and thyme
1/3 cup gouda cheese, crumbled
2 slices of the most expensive bread you can find, don't cheap out on this

Pre-heat the oven to 350 F.
Cut the tomatoes in half. Sprinkle the tomatoes with salt, pepper, and thyme. Drizzle with olive oil. Roast the tomatoes at 350 F in a non-stick whatever for approximately one hour. Then proceed as if you were making a boring grilled cheese for a one-night stand who won't take a hint.

Blue Cheese Pony Express

2 slices white bread
1/4 cup blue cheese, crumbled
1/4 cup diced onion
1 clove garlic, minced
1/4 cup pink cabbage or leftover coleslaw, shredded
1 teaspoon olive oil

Sauté the onions, garlic, and cabbage/coleslaw until onions are caramelized. Add the blue cheese and stir until combined. Then drop it on your bread and fry it normal. Do not serve this to people who don't like blue cheese. They will turn irate.

Italian Gangster Sandwich

2 slices white bread
1 slice mortadella (Italian baloney)
2 slices provolone
4 slices pickled red peppers

Mortadella is like baloney made by somebody who cares. Like the difference between a toy train made in China and a toy train made at the North Pole. I've been drinking craft beer since noon. It's true what they say. A lot of it tastes like crap.

Gandalf Grilled Cheese

2 slices multi-grain bread
3 or 4 sage leaves
2 slices fontina cheese
1 tablespoon garlic butter

Fry the sage leaves in garlic butter until crispy. People will ask you what that amazing smell is. Tell them it's level 20 magic herbs. Sandwich the fried sage leaves and fry sandwich normally. Refer to the section called Cooking Instructions for Dummies if you've forgotten how to do this.

Mediterranean Grilled Cheese

2 slices white bread
6 slices zucchini, grilled
2 tablespoons hummus
1/3 cup grated mozzarella cheese

This is a grilled cheese you don't want to drown in ketchup. Might go better with garlic sauce. You can find garlic sauce at a store that sells garlic sauce.

Zeus's Favorite Sandwich

2 slices white bread
1/4 cup chopped feta cheese
1/4 cup grated cheddar cheese
1 tablespoon red onion, chopped
1 plum tomato, sliced

Zeus doesn't often visit Earth to pick up ladies and eat sandwiches, but when he does, this the grilled cheese he'll throw at the bouncer's face to start a bar fight.

Jalapeno Popper

2 slices white bread
4 tablespoons cream cheese
1 tablespoon pickled jalapeno peppers, diced
1 teaspoon sour cream
1/4 cup shredded Monterey Jack cheese

Combine everything that isn't made out of bread, then spoon it onto the bread, then fry it regular like.

Roast Beast

2 slices white bread
1/3 cup brie cheese
2 slices roast beef
1 tablespoon Dijon mustard

You can swap out the roast beef for jungle boar.

On the Subject of Hamburger Buns

Some people ask me: "Is it okay to use hamburger buns instead of slices of white bread?"
This is a silly question. If you prefer hamburger buns to white bread then you should use hamburger buns.
These recipes are not bonus Commandments etched into stone by the Guy upstairs.
In fact, I recommend always doing whatever the hell you want to do.
That's freedom, baby.
If you want to swap out all the cheese for tofu, then do it. Just don't write a book about it. Books are my thing. Get your own thing.

This Recipe is Gonna Blow Your Mind (Macaroni and Ground Beef)

4 slices white bread
1 box of macaroni and cheese, or Kraft Dinner if you can get it
1/2 pound ground beef
1/2 teaspoon Italian seasoning
1/2 cup grated cheddar cheese, divided

Okay so here's what you do. First you cook your macaroni according to the instructions on the box. Don't make those dumb little tweaks you usually make, like extra butter or bonus milk. Listen to the box. Meanwhile, brown your ground beef in a skillet over medium-high heat. Drain the excess fat. When your macaroni is finished, dump the ground beef, cheddar cheese, and Italian seasoning into the macaroni pot and stir well.

Spoon your creation onto two slices of bread and fry it normal. Don't make this recipe too often or you'll get super fat and people won't invite you to amusement parks.

Hot Dogs and Maple Syrup

2 slices white bread
2 tablespoons maple syrup
2 tablespoons cream cheese
1 hot dog, cooked and chopped
1/3 cup grated cheddar cheese

This is a recipe you feed to people who say things like: "Grilled cheese is boring." Tell them Gordon Ramsay made this recipe and features it in his Vegas restaurant. (This is not true.)

Leftover Pizza Grilled Cheese

2 slices white bread
1 slice leftover pizza
1/4 cup grated cheddar cheese

Scrape your cheese and all the pizza toppings onto your bread and fry it regular. Discard scraped pizza dough or chop it up and feed it to your dog. Dogs digest things easier if they're tiny pieces. Ever heard of kibble?

Green Olives and Mozzarella

2 slices white bread
1/3 cup shredded mozzarella cheese
10 green olives, pitted and sliced

This is a great sandwich to ease the suffering of drinking too much alcohol. This is because olives have lots of sodium, also they're delicious.

Big City Waffle

2 frozen toaster-style waffles, thawed
1/3 cup grated cheddar cheese
4 slices crispy bacon

Drown in maple syrup and make a doctor's appointment to check for diabetes. Have fun trying to get butter into all the little waffle cracks.
This sandwich hardly ever fries properly unless you squish it with a spatula.

Canadian Senator

2 slices expensive bread
1 pear, sliced
1/3 cup chopped cold camembert
2 soda crackers, crushed

This grilled cheese is best when pears are out-of-season and super expensive. Make one sandwich and throw the expensive loaf of bread in the garbage. Write it off as an expense. If you run into legal trouble call Donald Bayne.

Fat Hawaiian

2 slices white bread
1/2 cup diced pineapple chunks
1/3 cup shredded habanero cheese
2 slices deli ham, chopped

You ever notice how the indigenous Hawaiian people are never in the news? What's up with that?

Somebody Left a Baguette at my Party and I Don't Know What to do with it

1 random baguette
onions, to taste
gruyere cheese, to taste
olive oil, for caramelizing

Slice your baguette in half or into little circles. (Do what makes you happy.)
Caramelize the onions in a skillet with some olive oil.
Spoon the onions and gruyere cheese onto your bread.
Melt your open-faced grilled cheese sandwiches under the broiler (high heat.)
If somebody asks what it's called, tell them it's French. Then ask why they didn't bring any wine.

Brie and Marmalade

2 slices cinnamon-raisin bread
1/3 cup brie
2 tablespoons orange marmalade

My ex-girlfriend liked this grilled cheese because it sounds fancy. (Personal I think it's disgusting, just like her ugly face.)
I'm not bitter I'm just misunderstood.

Apples, Bacon, and Brie

2 slices white bread
4 strips bacon, crispy
1/3 cup brie cheese
1 apple, skinned and diced

Every year at Christmas my mother used to serve fruit salad and a cheese platter for brunch. She always bought too much brie so we turned it into sandwiches. You can swap the apple for a 1/2 cup of fruit salad if you think you're a bad enough dude.

Obese American Doughnut

1 doughnut that doesn't have any crap on it
1/3 cup grated cheddar cheese
nacho cheese sauce, for dipping

If you buy a donut with icing on it you're gonna make a mess when you try and fry it regular.
I borrowed the idea for this sandwich from that Food Network TV show where a fat guy drives around America visiting unique restaurants and trying to get heart disease.

Pulled Pork Grilled Cheese

2 slices crusty white bread
1/2 cup cooked chicken, shredded
1/2 cup barbecue sauce
1/3 cup grated cheddar cheese

Serve this to people you're trying to gas light. They'll try and replicate it, but won't be able to get the taste right. Eventually they go insane.
The best chicken is the one you've smoked yourself, but those rotisserie chickens they sell at the grocery store works fine. You could also use leftover chicken from Swiss Chalet. Just make sure you can plausibly pass it off as pulled pork.

You ever buy too much breakfast at McDonald's?

Instead of throwing it in the garbage, put it in the fridge. The next morning scrape it all between two pieces of bread, 1/3 cup of grated cheddar cheese and then fry it regular.
This will taste like ride across America in a Greyhound bus.

Teriyaki Grilled Cheese

2 slices white bread
1/3 cup grated Monterey Jack cheese
2 tablespoons teriyaki sauce

Throw some leftover chicken or steak in there if you're looking for protein because you're a gym rat who wants big muscles to impress the ladies. Do 30 pushups while it's frying. You can do it. You're a tough hombre.

Green Herbs and White Cheese

2 slices white bread
1/3 cup mozzarella cheese
2 tablespoons grated parmesan cheese
1 slice provolone cheese
A pinch of every green herb you can think of
1 clove garlic, minced

Oregano, basil, whatever. Just go nuts. Make it different every time so nobody can learn your secret recipe. Combine everything that isn't bread, then spoon it onto your bread, then fry it regular.

Chipotle Meat

2 slices white bread
1/2 cup pre-cooked meat
3 tablespoons chipotle barbecue sauce
1/3 cup gruyere cheese

Chicken is probably your best choice, but you could use anything you hit with your car. Just add more BBQ sauce if you're using one of the gnarlier meats, like beaver or turkey vulture.

On the Subject of Beavers

Everybody thinks beavers are these cute little animals. They're actually super annoying if you live in the country. They dam swamps and ponds and flood your road. At night they chop down the trees and ruin your waterfront. Sometimes they don't even drag the trees back to their stupid beaver huts. They just leave them there like murder victims

Beavers are an obnoxious gym-bro that nobody invited to the party who gets super wasted and rips off your fridge door and uses it as a toboggan.

If I ever catch one I'm gonna turn it into a hat.

Vegan Grilled Cheese

2 slices white bread
2 slices vegan cheese
2 tablespoons vegan mayonnaise

Vegan cheese and vegan mayo are the only veganized products that don't taste like a dumpster fire. The cheese doesn't have any protein because it's usually made with coconut oil, but at least it's not vegan sausage. Vegan sausage makes me want to invest in a lab-grown meat company.

Blueberries and Maple Syrup

2 slices white bread
1/3 cup low-fat mozzarella cheese
1/3 cup of fresh blueberries
2 tablespoons maple syrup

My grandfather always said that eating blueberries prevents you from turning into a retard when you get old.
He died of cancer so I guess it works.

Actually a Pulled Pork Sandwich

2 slices white bread
1/2 cup shredded pulled pork
1/4 cup guacamole
1/3 cup grated cheddar cheese
 2 tablespoons Sriracha hot sauce, or to taste

Can you tell I eat a lot of guacamole? If you use enough lime juice it can last for up to a week in your fridge.

You know you can swap out some of these ingredients, right?

It's not like there's a thug standing behind you with a .38 snubnosed revolver saying "Follow the recipe or I'll plug ya."

Personally I like things a bit spicier so I use extra-hot cheddar cheese filled with jalapeno and habanero and red pepper flakes and stuff like that.

You know what I learned the other day? Cheddar is cheese curds pressed into a block. That's why fresh cheddar is squeaky like the curds. It's same thing. What a world.

Also, garlic cheese curds are pretty good. I only bought them because I was flirting with the cashier but they turned out alright.

German Drunkfest

1 pretzel roll, sliced in half
1 bratwurst or polish sausage, cooked and casing removed
1 clump of sauerkraut, or to taste
1/3 cup gruyere cheese
salt and black pepper, to taste
2 tablespoons hot mustard
1-12 German beers, for drinking

Personally I wouldn't go with a stout beer for this grilled cheese. Your best bet is amber because it pairs nicely with the pretzel roll.
Speaking of amber, is it just me, or was *Jurassic World* was just alright? *Jurassic Park*, the first one, is still the best I think.
Fun fact, the guy who wrote the screenplay to *Jurassic Park* also wrote the book.

Ghetto Lobster Roll

2 slices white bread
2 slices provolone
1/4 cup grated parmesan cheese
1/2 cup frozen pre-cooked lobster chunks, thawed and shredded
1-2 tablespoons mayonnaise

Impress your dumb little buddies by serving them lobster. Don't tell them the lobster meat was from a frozen can and only cost like five bucks.

Anchovies and Mozzarella

2 slices white bread
3 tablespoons pizza sauce
1/3 cup mozzarella cheese
2 anchovy fillets, diced

If you don't cut the anchovies with the pizza sauce you're gonna filibuster the sandwich. Throw some pepperoni in there if you got it. Once a pepperoni package is opened it never makes it to the best-before date.
Just one of those things, I guess.

Sides to Serve with Grilled Cheese

Garlic dill pickles
Olives
Kraft Dinner (Macaroni and Cheese)
French fries/Poutine
Potato chips
Salad (LOL)

If you haven't tried poutine, do yourself a favor and buy a can of beef gravy, some frozen French fries, and a package of white cheese curds. Cook the fries, heat the gravy.
Dump the fries in a bowl, cover with gravy, and then add cheese curds.
Welcome to Canada. Come for the legal marijuana (*coming soon*), but stay for the poutine.
Obviously a real poutine you get from a chip truck in small town on the side of the highway in Quebec is gonna be better than the recipe I just gave you, but it's a start. Also, this is a book about grilled cheese, so really, this is just a bonus.
Some people use chicken gravy. Don't make eye contact with them.
Fact: KFC uses chicken gravy on their poutine.
Fact: Colonel Sanders died of leukemia.
Coincidence? I don't think so.

Instant Pot BBQ Pork

Ingredients

1 tablespoon dry mustard
1 1/2 tablespoons smoked paprika
1 tablespoon onion powder
1/2 teaspoon cayenne pepper
1 teaspoon cumin ground
1 teaspoon garlic powder
1 tablespoon brown sugar
1 teaspoon black pepper ground
2 teaspoons salt
2 racks baby back pork ribs (about 3 to 4 lbs)
4 cups apple juice
1/4 cup apple cider vinegar
2 tablespoons liquid smoke
1/2 cup bbq sauces store bought
1/2 cup ketchup
1/4 cup whiskey
1/4 cup brown sugar
2 tablespoons Worcestershire sauce
1 tablespoon liquid smoke

Directions

Prepare the dry rub by combining all the dry rub ingredients together in a small bowl.

Take away the membrane from the trunk of the ribs with a paper towel.

Season the infant back ribs with the dry rub generously on both sides.

Place the ribs within the Instant Pot, taking a stand and wrapping around the moment Pot.

Pour the apple juice, apple cider vinegar and liquid smoke inside the Instant pot, no need to stir. Close the lid (follow the manufacturer's guide for instructions about how to close the instant pot lid). Set the moment Pot to the Meat/Stew setting and set the timer to 20 minutes.

Once the Instant Pot cycle is complete, wait until the natural release cycle is complete, should take about quarter-hour. Follow the manufacturer's guide for quick release, if in a rush. Carefully unlock and take away the lid from the moment pot.

While the ribs are cooking prepare the BBQ sauce. In a small saucepan add all of the BBQ sauce ingredients and stir to mix. Simmer on low heat for about 20 to 25 minutes, the sauce should reduce a bit.

Carefully take away the ribs from the moment Pot and place them onto a baking sheet. Brush them generously with the prepared BBQ sauce on both sides and place beneath the broiler for about 5 minutes. Keep carefully the door to your oven open while broiling the ribs and monitor them, because they could burn quickly.

Serve with leftover BBQ sauce.

Kansas City Style Pork Ribs

Ingredients

2 slabs pork spare ribs, 3 pounds each
kansas city barbeque sauce, recipe follows
2 cups brown sugar
1/2 cup dry mustard
1 tablespoon cayenne pepper
1 tablespoon smoked paprika
1 tablespoon garlic powder
1 tablespoon onion powder
1 tablespoon salt
2 teaspoons freshly ground black pepper
2 tablespoons vegetable oil
1 2/3 1 (about 2/3 cup)small onions, finely diced
3 cups water
1 cup (2 (6-ounce) cans) tomato paste
1/2 cup brown sugar
2/3 cup apple cider vinegar
1/4 cup molasses
1/2 teaspoon cayenne pepper
1/4 teaspoon smoked paprika
1 teaspoon salt

1 teaspoon freshly ground black pepper

Directions

Take away the thin white membrane from the bone-side of the ribs. Mix together the brown sugar, dry mustard, cayenne, paprika, garlic powder, onion powder, salt and pepper in a small bowl. Massage the rub in to the ribs and let sit for one hour or up to overnight.

If cooking on the grill, place the ribs meat-side down next to medium-hot coals that are about 225 degrees F. The indirect heat will cook them slower, making them tender. Allow to cook for one hour. Turn ribs every half hour and baste with the Kansas City Barbeque Sauce. Cook before ribs are tender, about three to four 4 hours.

If cooking indoors, place in a roasting pan with a rack. Slather the ribs with the Kansas City Barbeque Sauce and tent a bit of aluminum foil over them. In a preheated 350 degrees F. oven, place the ribs, basting with the sauce every 30 minutes and removing the foil going back 30 minutes and cooking until fork tender, about 2 1/2 to 3 hours.

In a small sauce pot on medium-high heat, heat the oil and add the onion, cooking until translucent.

Add the remaining ingredients in a huge bowl and mix together. Increase sauce pan and let simmer for 30 to 45 minutes. Use to baste the pork spare ribs.

No-Fuss Baked Baby Back Ribs

Ingredients

1 cup soy sauce
1 cup Worcestershire sauce
1 tablespoon liquid smoke
1 tablespoon brown sugar
1 teaspoon ground ginger
pinch kosher salt and freshly ground black pepper
6 racks baby back ribs (about 2 pounds each), membranes removed
2 cups yellow mustard
2 cups dark brown sugar
1 1/2 cups apple cider vinegar
1 cup granulated sugar
2 heaping teaspoons garlic powder
2 heaping teaspoons onion powder
1/2 teaspoon smoked paprika
ounce one 15- can tomato sauce
kosher salt and freshly ground black pepper

Directions

For the ribs: Mix together the soy sauce, Worcestershire, liquid smoke, brown sugar, ginger, pinch of salt and 1 1/2 teaspoons pepper in a sizable measuring cup. Arrange the ribs in a roasting pan, hotel pan or baking dish large enough to fit them all. Pour the marinade over the ribs. Toss and flip until all of the ribs are coated. Marinate 1 hour at room temperature or refrigerate up to overnight.

Preheat the oven to 250 degrees F. Line 3 rimmed baking sheets with aluminum foil.

Place 2 racks of ribs on each baking sheet, meat-side up. Brush with any remaining marinade left behind in the roasting pan. Cover with more foil. Bake for 2 hours.

For the Carolina moppin' sauce: Meanwhile, put the mustard, brown sugar, vinegar, granulated sugar, garlic powder, onion powder, smoked paprika and tomato sauce in a sizable saucepan and whisk until completely combined. Season lightly with salt and pepper. Place over medium-high heat and bring to a boil. Reduce to medium-low and simmer until thickened, about 1 hour.

Uncover the ribs and drain off the fat, reserving for another use (see Cook's Note). Mop or brush the sauce on both sides, returning the ribs to meat-side up. Improve the oven to 300 degrees F and bake the ribs, uncovered, before meat is tender and the sauce begins to caramelize, about 1 more hour.

Mop the ribs again on both sides. Improve the oven to 375 degrees F and bake the ribs, uncovered and adding more sauce as it absorbs, before meat gets brown and caramelized, about one hour more. Cut the ribs into individual pieces. Use the remaining sauce for serving, or retain in the refrigerator for later use.

Oven Barbecue Pork Ribs Recipe

Ingredients

for the spice rub:
1/3 cup paprika (2 1/4 ounces; 65g)
1/4 cup dark brown sugar (2 ounces; 55g)
1/4 cup diamond crystal kosher salt (1 1/2 ounces; 40g); for table salt, use about half as much by volume or the same weight
2 tablespoons whole yellow mustard seed (1/4 ounce; 8g)
2 tablespoons granulated garlic powder (1/4 ounce; 8g)
1 tablespoon onion powder (1/8 ounce; 4g)
1 tablespoon dried oregano (1/8 ounce; 4g)
1 tablespoon whole coriander seed (1/8 ounce; 4g)
1 teaspoon whole cumin seed
1 teaspoon red pepper flakes
1 teaspoon freshly ground black pepper
for the sauce (if using):

1 medium yellow onion, grated on the large holes of a box grater
1 1/2 cups (350ml) ketchup
2 tablespoons (30ml) spicy brown mustard
1/3 cup (80ml) dark molasses
1/4 cup (60ml) Worcestershire sauce
1/4 cup (60ml) apple cider vinegar
3/4 teaspoon (4ml) wright's or colgin liquid hickory smoke

for the ribs:
2 whole racks st. louis–cut pork ribs (about 2 1/2 pounds/1kg each)
1 teaspoon (5ml) wright's or colgin liquid hickory smoke, plus more if needed

Directions

1. For the Spice Rub: Employed in batches, combine paprika, brown sugar, salt, mustard seed, garlic powder, onion powder, oregano, coriander seed, cumin seed, red pepper flakes, and black pepper in a spice grinder and reduce to an excellent powder.

2. For the Sauce (if using): Combine 3 tablespoons spice rub, grated onion, ketchup, mustard, molasses, Worcestershire sauce, vinegar, and liquid smoke in a medium saucepan and whisk thoroughly. Bring to a

bare simmer and cook until reduced and thickened, about 20 minutes. Reserve.

3. For the Ribs: Take away the papery membrane on the trunk of the ribs, utilizing a paper towel or kitchen towel to grip it, pulling it away in one piece. Rub ribs generously on all sides with spice rub mixture. (Reserve 3 tablespoons of spice rub if making dry-style ribs.)

4. Sprinkle ribs around with 1 teaspoon liquid smoke, then rub in with hands for even coverage. If ribs don't smell smoky enough, sparingly rub in more liquid smoke. Wrap each rib rack in plastic and refrigerate for at least 2 and up to 8 hours.

5. Preheat oven to 250°F (120°C) and set rack in center position; set a wire rack in a rimmed baking sheet. Remove and discard plastic from the rib racks, then wrap each rib rack in foil, sealing it tightly, and set on prepared baking sheet. Bake ribs for 2 hours. Remove and discard foil. Return to oven, meaty side up, and continue steadily to cook until a toothpick or skewer could be pushed into meat with minimal resistance, about 1 1/2 hours longer. (Cooking times can vary quite a bit based on the specific size of rib racks and the oven being used.)

6. TO COMPLETE: Increase oven to 500°F (260°C). Meanwhile, rub racks with remaining 3 tablespoons spice rub (if making them dry-style) or brush with sauce (if using). Go back to oven and cook, meaty side up, until well browned, 5 to 10 minutes. Divide ribs

between bones, if desired; serve, passing additional sauce at the table, if using.

Prize Winning Baby Back Ribs Recipe

Ingredients

---

1 tablespoon ground cumin
1 tablespoon chili powder
1 tablespoon paprika
salt and pepper to taste
3 pounds baby back pork ribs
1 cup barbeque sauces

Directions

Step one 1 Preheat a gas grill for high temperature, or arrange charcoal briquettes on one side of the barbeque. Lightly oil the grate. Advertisement

Step two 2 In a little jar, combine cumin, chili powder, paprika, salt, and pepper. Close the lid, and shake to combine.

Step three 3 Trim the membrane sheath from the back of each rack. Run a little, sharp knife between the membrane and each rib, and snip off the membrane as much as possible. Sprinkle as a lot of the rub onto both sides of the ribs as desired. To avoid the ribs from becoming too dark and spicy, usually do not thoroughly rub the spices in to the ribs. Store the unused portion of the spice mix for future use.

Step 4 Place aluminum foil on lower rack to capture drippings and prevent flare-ups. Lay the ribs on the top rack of the grill (away from the coals, if you are using briquettes). Reduce gas heat to low, close lid, and leave undisturbed for one hour. Usually do not lift the lid at all.

Step 5 Brush ribs with barbecue sauce, and grill an additional five minutes. Serve ribs as whole rack, or cut between each rib bone and pile individually on a platter.

Recipe: Oven-Baked Barbecue Ribs

Ingredients

5 pounds beef back ribs
1 cup canola or vegetable oil
1/2 cup cider vinegar
3 tablespoons packed brown sugar
1 tablespoon plus 1 teaspoon soy sauce
1 tablespoon Worcestershire sauce
1 teaspoon garlic powder
1/2 teaspoon onion powder
1/2 teaspoon kosher salt
2 tablespoons unsalted butter
1 1/2 cups ketchup
1/3 cup Worcestershire sauce
1/4 cup steak sauces or marinade (i use allegra)
2 tablespoons unsulfured molasses
1/2 teaspoon onion powder
1/8 teaspoon liquid smoke
freshly ground pepper

Directions

For the marinade

Whisk all ingredients together until well combined. In a sizable baking dish, pour marinade over ribs and refrigerate, basting occasionally, for at the least 2 hours, but preferably overnight.

Preheat oven to 300°. Cover baking dish with aluminum foil and cook ribs for 2 hours.

Increase the oven temperature to 350°. Take away the aluminum foil and baste ribs with barbecue sauce. Continue cooking for 45 minutes, basting with sauce every a quarter-hour. The ribs should easily separate with a knife and the meat ought to be fall off the bone tender.

Serve ribs with remaining barbecue sauce on the side.

For the barbecue sauce

In a little saucepan, melt butter over medium heat. Add remaining ingredients, whisking to mix. Bring to a boil, then reduce heat to a simmer. Allow to cook until thick, approximately ten minutes.

Rhubarb-Apricot Barbecued Chicken

Ingredients

1 tablespoon olive oil
1 cup finely chopped sweet onions
1 garlic clove, minced
2 cups chopped fresh or frozen rhubarb
3/4 cup ketchup
2/3 cup water
1/3 cup apricot preserves
1/4 cup cider vinegar
1/4 cup molasses
1 tablespoon honey dijon mustard
2 teaspoons finely chopped chipotle pepper in adobo sauces
5 teaspoons barbecue seasonings, divided
1 1/4 teaspoons 1-1/4 salt, divided
3/4 teaspoon pepper, divided
12 chicken drumsticks (about 4 pounds)

Directions

In a big saucepan, heat oil over medium heat. Add onion; cook and stir until tender, 4-6 minutes. Add garlic; cook 1 minute longer. Stir in rhubarb, ketchup, water, preserves, vinegar, molasses, mustard, chipotle pepper, 1 teaspoon barbecue seasoning, 1/4 teaspoon salt and 1/4 teaspoon pepper. Bring to a boil. Reduce heat; simmer, uncovered, until rhubarb is tender, 8-10 minutes. Puree rhubarb mixture using an immersion blender, or cool slightly and puree in a blender. Reserve 2 cups sauce for serving.

Meanwhile, in a little bowl, mix the rest of the barbecue seasoning, salt and pepper; sprinkle over chicken. On a lightly oiled grill rack, grill chicken, covered, over indirect medium heat a quarter-hour. Turn; grill until a thermometer reads 170°-175°, 15-20 minutes longer, brushing occasionally with remaining sauce. Serve with reserved sauce.

Slow Cooker Barbecue Ribs

Ingredients

4 pounds pork baby back ribs
salt and pepper
garlic powder, onion powder (about 1/2 teaspoon each)
2 cups of your favorite barbecue sauce
1 cup ketchup
1/2 cup packed brown sugar
4 tablespoons red wine vinegar
2 teaspoons Worcestershire sauce
2 teaspoons dried oregano
1 tablespoon optional liquid smoke if you like a smokey flavor
dash optional hot sauces my bbq sauce was spicy enough already

Directions

Preheat oven to 400 degrees.

Place ribs in a shallow baking dish and season with salt, pepper, garlic powder, and onion powder. Bake for quarter-hour and then turn over and bake for 15 more minutes. Drain fat.

In a medium bowl combine BBQ sauce, ketchup, brown sugar, vinegar, Worcestershire, oregano, and liquid smoke and hot sauce if desired.

Place ribs in a large slow cooker (at least 6 quart). I curled mine around nevertheless, you can cut them in two if you want to. Pour sauce at the top and cook on low for 6-8 hours or until tender.

If you want to carmelize your bbq sauce put them back the oven for a quarter-hour at 400 degrees. Totally your preference though.

Southern Grilled Barbecued Ribs Recipe

Ingredients

4 pounds baby back pork ribs
2/3 cup water
1/3 cup red wine vinegar
1 cup ketchup
1 cup water
1/2 cup cider vinegar
1/3 cup Worcestershire sauce
1/4 cup prepared mustard
4 tablespoons butter
1/2 cup packed brown sugar
1 teaspoon hot pepper sauces
teaspoon ? salt

Directions

Step 1 1 Preheat oven to 350 degrees F (175 degrees C). Place ribs in two 10x15 inch roasting pans. Pour water and burgandy or merlot wine vinegar right into a bowl, and stir. Pour diluted vinegar over ribs and cover with foil. Bake in the preheated oven for 45 minutes. Baste the ribs with their juices halfway through cooking. Advertisement

Step two 2 In a medium saucepan, mix together ketchup, water, vinegar, Worcestershire sauce, mustard, butter, brown sugar, hot pepper sauce, and salt; bring to a boil. Reduce heat to low, cover, and simmer barbeque sauce for one hour.

Step three 3 Preheat grill for medium heat.

Step 4 Lightly oil preheated grill. Transfer ribs from the oven to the grill, discarding cooking liquid. Grill over medium heat for a quarter-hour, turning ribs once. Baste ribs generously with barbeque sauce, and grill 8 minutes. Turn ribs, baste again with barbeque sauce, and grill 8 minutes.

Spicy and Sticky Baby Back Ribs

Ingredients

1 cup dark brown sugar
3 tablespoons kosher salt
1 tablespoon dry mustard
1 tablespoon ground fennel
1 tablespoon freshly ground black pepper
1 tablespoon cayenne pepper
1 tablespoon sweet smoked paprika
4 racks baby back ribs (about 2 1/2 pounds each), membrane removed from the underside of each rack
1 tablespoon unsalted butter
1 small onion, minced
3 garlic cloves, minced
1 1/2 teaspoons dried thyme
1 cup ketchup
1 cup cider vinegar
1 cup beef broth
1/4 cup hot sauce
1/4 cup Worcestershire sauce
2 tablespoons unsulfured molasses

Directions

Step 1

In a small bowl, combine the brown sugar, salt, mustard, fennel, black pepper, cayenne and paprika. On 2 large rimmed baking sheets, sprinkle the spice mix all around the ribs, pressing and patting it. Cover with foil and refrigerate overnight.

Step 2

Preheat the oven to 250°. Pour off any liquid on the baking sheets, cover the ribs with foil and roast for about 3 hours, until the meat is tender however, not falling off the bone. Pour off any liquid on the baking sheets.

Step 3

Meanwhile, in a saucepan, melt the butter. Add the onion, garlic and thyme and cook over moderate heat until the onion is softened, about 5 minutes. Add the ketchup, vinegar, beef broth, hot sauce, Worcestershire sauce and molasses and bring to a boil. Simmer over low heat, stirring occasionally, until thickened, about 30 minutes.

Step 4

Preheat the broiler and position a rack 10 inches from heat. Brush the ribs liberally with the barbecue sauce and broil for about ten minutes, turning and brushing occasionally with the sauce, until well-browned and crispy in spots. Transfer the ribs to a work surface and let rest for five minutes. Cut in between the bones and mound the ribs on a platter. Pass any extra barbecue sauce privately.

Stickiest ever BBQ ribs with chive dip recipe

Ingredients

2 racks baby back pork ribs
2 cans cola
2 teaspoons toasted sesame seed(optional)
8 tbsp tomato ketchup
8 tbsp soft brown sugar
2 tbsp soy sauce
2 tbsp Worcestershire sauce
2 tbsp sweet chilli sauces
1 teaspoon paprika
300 ml pot half-fat soured cream
2 tbsp salad cream
bunch small chive, snipped
6 spring onions, sliced

Directions

Heat oven to 160C/140C fan/gas 3 and snugly fit the ribs right into a roasting tin. Pour over the cola and enough water to cover the ribs, then cover the tin tightly with foil. Roast for 2-3 hrs, turning halfway through, before ribs are really tender however, not falling apart.

Meanwhile, put all of the sauce ingredients in a small saucepan. Gently heat, then bubble for approximately 2 mins, stirring.

When the ribs are done, carefully lift each out from the tin and take a seat on kitchen paper to dry. Tip away the liquid and wipe out the tin. Put the dry ribs back in the tin and coat around with the sticky sauce. Cover and chill for at least 1 hr to marinate, but better still up to 24 hrs. Can be frozen at this time.

Mix the dip ingredients together and chill until prepared to serve.

Heat the barbecue and wait for the flames to die down, or heat oven to 220C/200C/gas 7. Add the ribs (in a roasting tin, if using the oven) and cook for 20 mins, turning occasionally, and basting often with remaining sauce. When ribs are sticky, hot through and crisping on the outside, slice to serve. Scatter with sesame seeds, if you like, and plate up with any remaining sticky sauce, warmed, and the chive dip.

Texas Pork Ribs Recipe

Ingredients

6 pounds pork spareribs
1 1/2 cups white sugar
1/4 cup salt
2 1/2 tablespoons ground black pepper
3 tablespoons sweet paprika
1 teaspoon cayenne pepper, or to taste
2 tablespoons garlic powder
5 tablespoons pan drippings
1/2 cup chopped onions
4 cups ketchup
3 cups hot water
4 tablespoons brown sugar
cayenne pepper to taste
salt and pepper to taste
1 cup wood chips, soaked

Directions

Step one 1 Clean the ribs, and trim away any extra fat. In a medium bowl, stir together the sugar, 1/4 cup salt, ground black pepper, paprika, 1 teaspoon cayenne pepper, and garlic powder. Coat ribs liberally with spice mix. Place the ribs in two 10x15 inch roasting pans, piling two racks of ribs per pan. Cover, and refrigerate for at least 8 hours. Advertisement

Step two 2 Preheat oven to 275 degrees F (135 degrees C). Bake uncovered for three to four 4 hours, or until the ribs are tender and almost fall apart.

Step three 3 Remove 5 tablespoons of drippings from underneath of the roasting pans, and place in a skillet over medium heat. Cook onion in pan drippings until lightly browned and tender. Stir in ketchup, and heat for 3 to 4 4 more minutes, stirring constantly. Next, mix in water and brown sugar, and season to taste with cayenne pepper, salt, and pepper. Reduce heat to low, cover, and simmer for 1 hour, adding water as essential to achieve desired thickness.

Step 4 Preheat grill for medium-low heat.

Step 5 When prepared to grill, add soaked wood chips to the coals or to the smoker box of a gas grill. Lightly oil grill grate. Place ribs on the grill two racks at a time so they are not crowded. Cook for 20 minutes, turning occasionally. Baste ribs with sauce during the last ten minutes of grilling, therefore the sauce does not burn.

The Best BBQ Chicken Breasts

Ingredients

4 boneless skinless chicken breasts
extra virgin olive oil
kosher salt , to taste
freshly ground black pepper , to taste
1/2 cup of your favorite bbq sauces

Directions

Prepare the grill for direct cooking at high heat (450°F). Brush the cooking grates clean.

Drizzle the chicken breasts with extra virgin olive oil and rub over the breasts. Season generously with kosher salt and freshly ground black pepper.

Place the chicken breasts on the hot grill. Cover and cook for 5-6 minutes or until they easily release from the grates. Flip the chicken and cook for 4-5 minutes longer. Baste the chicken breasts with BBQ sauce, flip and cook for 2 minutes on each side. Repeat on the other hand. Cook before breasts are firm to touch and opaque all the way through, registering 160°F internal temp (the temp will rise to 165°F as the chicken rests).

Transfer to a plate and cover with a bit of aluminum foil and let rest for 5 minutes. Serve with more BBQ sauce if desired.

The Ultimate Barbecued Chicken

Ingredients

2 quarts water water
2 tablespoons salt kosher salt
1/4 cup brown sugar brown sugar
2 cloves garlic garlic smashed with the side of a large knife
4 sprigs thyme fresh thyme
6 ounces chicken chicken legs and thighs still connected bone in skin on about 10 each
1 slice bacon bacon
1 bunch thyme fresh thyme
olive oil Extra-virgin olive oil
1/2 onion onion chopped
2 cloves garlic garlic chopped
2 cups ketchup ketchup
1/4 cup brown sugar brown sugar
1/4 cup molasses molasses
2 tablespoons white wine vinegar red or white wine vinegar
1 tablespoon dry mustard dry mustard
1 teaspoon cumin ground cumin
1 teaspoon paprika paprika or smoked paprika if available

black pepper Freshly ground black pepper

Directions

For the brine, in a mixing bowl combine the water, salt, sugar, garlic, and thyme. Transfer the brine to a 2-gallon sized re-sealable plastic bag. Add the chicken, close the bag and refrigerate 2 hours (if you have only got a quarter-hour, that's fine) to permit the salt and seasonings to penetrate the chicken.

Meanwhile, make the sauce. Wrap the bacon around the bunch of thyme and tie with kitchen twine which means you have a good bundle. Heat about 2 tablespoons of oil in a sizable saucepan over medium heat. Add the thyme and cook slowly three to four 4 minutes to render the bacon fat and present the sauce a good smoky taste. Add the onion and garlic and cook slowly without coloring for five minutes. Add the rest of the ingredients, give the sauce a stir, and turn heat right down to low. Cook slowly for 20 minutes to meld the flavors. After the sauce is performed cooking, remove about 1 1/2 cups of the sauce and reserve for serving with the chicken at the table. All of those other barbecue sauce will be utilized for basing the legs.

Preheat oven 375 degrees F.

Preheat a grill pan or a patio gas or charcoal barbecue to a medium heat. Take a few paper towels and fold them several times to produce a thick square. Blot a little amount of oil on the paper towel and carefully and quickly wipe the hot grates of the grill to make a nonstick surface. Take the chicken from the brine, pat it dry in some recoverable format towels. Arrange the chicken pieces on the preheated grill and cook, turn once mid-way, and cook for a complete of ten minutes. Transfer the grill marked chicken to a cookie sheet and place in the oven. Cook the chicken for 15 minutes, take it off from the oven and then brush liberally, coating every inch of the legs with the barbecue sauce and then return to the oven for 25 to 30 more minutes, basting the chicken for another time half way through remaining cooking time. Serve with extra sauce.

The Ultimate Barbecued Ribs

Ingredients

2 slabs baby back ribs (about 3 pounds)
kosher salt and freshly ground black pepper
extra-virgin olive oil
2 bacon slices
4 sprigs fresh thyme
1/2 onion
3 smashed garlic cloves
2 cups ketchup
1 cup peach preserves
2 tablespoons dijon mustard or 1 tablespoon dry mustard
2 tablespoons brown sugar
1/4 cup molasses
2 tablespoons red or white wine vinegar
1 teaspoon ground cumin
1 teaspoon ground paprika

Directions

Special equipment: Kitchen twine

Preheat the oven to 250 degrees F. Put the ribs on a baking sheet, season with salt and pepper and drizzle with essential olive oil. Stick them in the oven, and allow ribs bake, low and slow for 1 1/2 hours.

Meanwhile, make the sauce. Wrap the bacon around the center of the thyme sprigs and tie with kitchen twine so you have a good bundle. Heat 2 tablespoons oil in a big saucepan over medium heat. Add the thyme bundle and cook slowly for 3 to 4 4 minutes to render the bacon fat and give the sauce a nice smoky taste. Add the onion and garlic and cook slowly, without coloring, for 5 minutes. Add all the rest of the sauce ingredients, supply the sauce a stir, and turn heat right down to low. Cook slowly for 20 minutes to meld the flavors. Put some sauce in another bowl for basting, reserving the rest of the sauce for serving.

Baste the ribs with the sauce and let them continue cooking, basting twice more, for 30 more minutes. When the ribs are cooked, take them out of the oven. You can let them go out such as this until you're ready to eat.

When prepared to eat, preheat the broiler for 5 minutes and broil the ribs, basting with the sauce. They should become crisp and charred, about five minutes on each side. Pick the onion and garlic from the sauce and serve with ribs.

www.ingramcontent.com/pod-product-compliance
Lightning Source LLC
Chambersburg PA
CBHW071437070526
44578CB00001B/111